JN035242

Broad System of Ordering (BSO)

by
Keiichi Kawamura

Jusonbo
Tokyo

Broad System of Ordering (BSO)

© Keiichi Kawamura, 2023

Published by
Jusonbo Co. Ltd.
5-11-7 Koishikawa
Bunkyo-ku
Tokyo 112-0002
Japan

Tel: +81 (0)3 3868 7321
Fax: +81 (0)3 6801 5202
https://www.jusonbo.co.jp/

First published 2023

ISBN978-4-88367-382-7

Cover design by Miho Hara
Printed and bound in Japan by Marui-Kobunsha Corporation

Preface

The main part of this book was originally prepared as an article of "Broad System of Ordering (BSO)" for the free accessible online *ISKO Encyclopedia of Knowledge Organization* (IEKO) in response to their request. However, for a certain reason, I was compelled to withdraw the work from IEKO and later decided to publish it as a book. The book now ready for final editing is made up of three parts: Preface – Article for IEKO – Index, of which the first and the last were newly prepared. My previous work for IEKO, being also by request, was a biographical article of "Eric Coates" that was published in 2018 and updated in 2020.

There are three reasons why the article for IEKO should be published nonetheless. First, I cannot stop expressing my deep gratitude to those who supported me to bring the work to completion, which should be accompanied by a concrete outcome. Second, I must report on how I have met the requirements of the three anonymous referees who read the original manuscript carefully and made favourable comments and constructive suggestions to improve it. Third, I must come up to expectations made by those who looked forward to an encyclopaedia article on BSO, which was announced in advance on the webpage of IEKO.

I am grateful to Mr Eiichi Otsuka, the president of Jusonbo Co. Ltd., for undertaking the publication of the book.

Keiichi Kawamura
18th May 2023

Contents

List of figures and tables

Abstract

The Broad System of Ordering (BSO), first published in 1978, was developed to meet the requirements of the UNISIST programme for an international switching mechanism between systems using various indexing languages. Its broadness stemmed from an intention to link organizations and data collections and not to provide a detailed bibliographic system. As an ordering system BSO has inherited some of the traditions of library classification, but it also incorporates many features drawn from post-1945 classification theory which have not previously found expression together in completed general classification schemes. Being a broad ordering system, BSO was expected to serve other purposes besides the original switching role. This encyclopaedia article gives a comprehensive, exact and intelligible description of BSO.

1. Introduction

The Broad System of Ordering (BSO) was constructed at the Fédération Internationale de Documentation (FID) in association with the United Nations Educational, Scientific and Cultural Organization (UNESCO) in the framework of the UNISIST programme (see Endnote 1). It was intended as a switching mechanism for various indexing languages. The project was instituted by a predecessor of the FID/BSO Panel in 1973, and the first hard copy publication was released in 1978 as the BSO 3rd revision (Coates, Lloyd and Simandl 1978b). In form it was a non-explicitly faceted classification of about 4,000 terms. *The BSO Manual* (Coates, Lloyd and Simandl 1979a) gave a more extended treatment of the topics briefly touched upon in the BSO Introduction and included a specimen file of 750 directory entries of real life specialized organizations and secondary information services.

In the first half of the 1980s, following the publication of French version of the BSO 3rd revision (Coates, Lloyd and Simandl 1981a), two field tests of BSO were carried out. The first was the BSO Switching Test of 1981, and the second was the BSO Referral Test of 1982/83. In the second half of the 1980s, under the Panel's plans for the future (Coates 1986), revision of BSO was proposed, based largely upon the findings and experience of the two field tests. However, in 1990, when the promotion of the revised BSO was about to begin, BSO lost the support of FID (Fédération Internationale d'Information et de Documentation, 1986-2002, dissolved) and UNESCO, because of their financial crises. In 1991 the BSO Panel, which had taken over the copyright of BSO, released the revised BSO containing about 6,800 terms in machine-readable form on a set of three 3.5 inch disks (Coates et al. 1991a; see Endnotes 2 and 3).

In December 1992 BSO was incorporated as the BSO Panel Ltd in the United Kingdom. While BSO was developed in the framework of the UNISIST programme, the scheme in many respects reflected the work of the Classification Research Group (CRG) in London. This owed much to the efforts of Eric Coates who was one of the original members of the CRG and played a major part in constructing and testing BSO. In 2000 BSO came under the management of the University College London, School of Library, Archive and Information Studies (UCL/SLAIS, now the Department of Information Studies) which was the base of the CRG. They set up a website for BSO, and an updated version of the machine-readable form of the BSO 4th revision has been made available online free of charge (UCL/SLAIS 2000).

A bibliography of BSO was compiled (Kawamura 2011). It shows that BSO was expected to serve other purposes besides the original switching role. This is due to the fact that BSO has a dual property: a switching language for various indexing languages in the framework of the UNISIST programme and a new general classification incorporating many features drawn from the classification theory that the CRG developed. There were meanderings until BSO was realized, which was unavoidable for the first practical attempt at a universal switching language. For this reason this encyclopaedia article on BSO begins with a description of its prehistory.

2. Idea of a switching language and projects for an Intermediate Lexicon

Anticipation in the middle and late 1960s that information storage and retrieval would be increasingly mechanized led to the idea that a universal indexing language for mediating purposes might shortly be needed. For mainly economic reasons, interconnection of individual local indexing languages by means of a switching or mediating language was envisaged on the model given as Figure 1. A key feature of the model is the 'two-way equivalence or conversion tables' (see e.g. Horsnell 1975) in which the code for a given concept as rendered in one indexing language is coupled with the code for the same concept in another indexing language. The model is analogous to the common telephone network where each subscriber is not directly connected to every other subscriber, but all subscribers are connected to a telephone exchange.

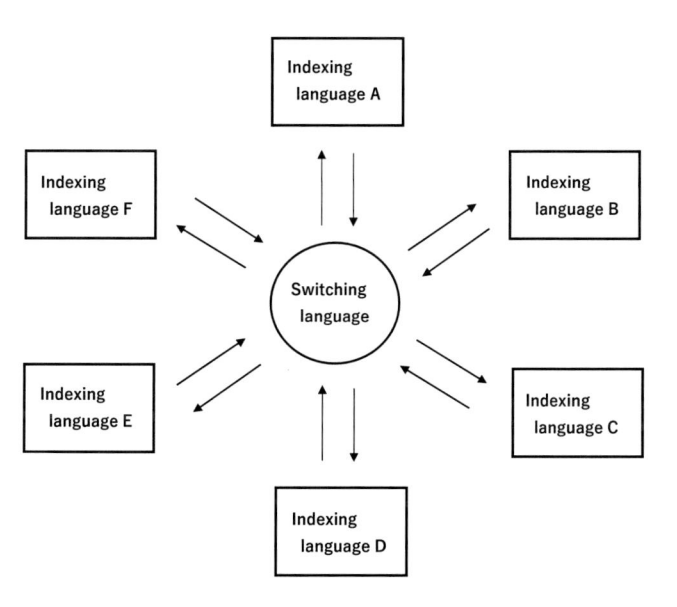

Figure 1: Networking model of interconnection of local indexing languages by means of a switching language

In 1963 a pioneering work to study a possible switching language was initiated by the Groupe d'Etude sur l'Information Scientifique (GEIS) headed by Jean-Claude Gardin, Marseilles, which was a unit of the Centre National de la Recherche Scientifique (CNRS) in France. The work included a project to develop an Intermediate Lexicon ('Lexique intermédiaire' in French) to permit easy inter-conversion between controlled vocabulary lists used for indexing literature in the field of documentation and library science. The project was called "Documentation of documentation", and two international conferences were held in Marseilles in 1965 and 1968. There were eight and fifteen participants respectively at these conferences from eight countries: Belgium, Denmark, France, Poland, Sweden, United Kingdom (UK), United States of America (USA) and West Germany. One prominent figure among the participants from abroad was Eric Coates (1968a; 1968b; 1970a) who was a representative of the CRG. It was recognized that there were about thirty indexing systems for the field of documentation, of which thirteen were selected for the project (GEIS 1967, 219-222). The project produced a list of twenty-five main divisions ('groupes' in French) of the Intermediate Lexicon. The outcome of the project was published both in French (GEIS 1968) and in English (Coates and Weeks 1969), and the Intermediate Lexicon was soon used experimentally for exchange of information between the GEIS and the Deutsche Gesellschaft für Dokumentation (DGD) in Frankfurt am Main (Gardin 1969a; Gardin 1969b).

The idea emanating from the GEIS was later given quantitative elaboration in a research study carried out by Verina Horsnell and her co-workers at the Polytechnic of North London School of Librarianship from 1971 to 1974. During the period further studies in the same area as that covered by the GEIS project were undertaken directed jointly by Jack Mills and Eric Coates. To determine the feasibility of such a device, a switching language named the Intermediate Lexicon for Information Science was developed and tested, supported by a grant from the British Library Research and Development Department (BLRDD, absorbing the former UK OSTI: Office for Scientific and Technical Information). Promising results were obtained that were quite favourable to the idea that information about the contents of documents could be switched between centres employing different indexing languages, without much greater information loss than was customary in information systems generally

(Horsnell 1974; Horsnell 1975). A second phase of research was carried out during the period from 1976 to 1978 (Horsnell and Merrett 1978).

3. UNISIST programme as an intergovernmental programme for cooperation

3.1 Three notable landmarks for clarification of the UNISIST requirements

As the idea of a switching language emanating from the GEIS was the only one of its kind available, it must have affected the thinking of members of the early bodies charged with the task of considering the global science information programme. There were three notable landmarks in the predevelopment of the global scientific information exchange, which later formed part of the UNISIST programme (intergovernmental programme for co-operation in the field of scientific and technological information).

The first landmark was a study project to consider the feasibility of such a programme, set up jointly by UNESCO and ICSU. In January 1967 a UNESCO/ICSU Central Committee was created, which included eight small working groups, of which the Working Group on Indexing and Classification was set up in 1968. The Working Group comprised Douglas Foskett (UK) as Chairman, André van der Laan (FID), Felix A. Sviridov (FID), Ingetraut Dahlberg (West Germany) and Péter Lázár (Hungary). The Working Group seem to have accepted the idea of a switching language, and they moved on to consider the next question, i.e. Could an existing classification or indexing language be used for the global scientific information network?

To assist the UNESCO/ICSU study of the feasibility of a World Science Information System (UNISIST), Aslib

(Association of Special Libraries and Information Bureaux, UK, later Association for Information Management) was commissioned to undertake a comparative study of general classification schemes in English as possible candidates for the switching language role. In their report the Aslib research team, under the direction of Brian Vickery, concluded that all the schemes were unacceptable, with the Universal Decimal Classification (UDC) emerging as the least defective (Vickery et al. 1969). The clear inference to be drawn from the report was that an entirely new indexing language should be set up for UNISIST purposes. However, the report pointed out that the detailed subject indexing requirements of UNISIST had by no means been fully defined. It was not possible to envisage with any useful degree of concreteness what the features of the new subject indexing language should be.

The second landmark was found in the *UNISIST: Study Report on the Feasibility of a World Science Information System* (UNESCO and ICSU 1971, 68 and 95). Jean-Claude Gardin was entrusted with the task of writing this final report based on the discussions of the UNESCO/ICSU Central Committee and the documentation supplied by its working groups. The following excerpts from the report and its preliminaries summed up the state of thinking at that time, both on the world science information network and on the subject indexing system appropriate to be attached to it:

"... a world science information system, considered as a flexible network evolving from an extension of voluntary co-operation of existing and future services is feasible" (from the Transmittal Memorandum addressed to Director-General of UNESCO and President of ICSU).

"... the goal, here, is not to devise a universal indexing language for all branches of science and technology".

The *UNISIST Study Report* went on to suggest that the

concept of standardization in indexing should be re-interpreted in the following manner:

"(a) restricting indexing standards to the most general classes (i.e. disciplines, sub-disciplines, etc.) for the purpose of broad subject categorization alone. (b) inferring metalinguistic standards from the comparison of different indexing vocabularies in given areas of science and technology, and using such standards as a tool for converting indexed representations from one semantic system to another. (c) observing recurrent formal properties in some or all information languages, from the point of view of semantic and syntactic structure".

The *UNISIST Study Report* looked forward to a system of "broad subject categories" for facilitating document exchange between different provinces of scientific documentation. It argued that the purpose of transfer was likely to be somewhat unsophisticated. Moreover, such a system might be employed:

"to characterize the holdings of libraries in a union catalog, to specify the field coverage of periodicals in a world register, to determine overlaps and duplications in the operational characteristics of information systems, or again as a broad filter in processing enquiries on information resources".

The *UNISIST Study Report* seemed to say that the internal indexing systems of the respective scientific provinces were never likely to be harmonized with each other to form a universally applicable indexing system. Therefore, for the world science information system, it was necessary to envisage a second superimposed layer of indexing activity, requiring a communications indexing language for linking the separated provinces.

The *UNISIST Study Report* considered whether any existing universal classification might meet the requirement for a switching language. Despite the views of the Aslib research team in their study, the *UNISIST Study Report* offered no conclusion on this issue. As might be expected, the views emanating from FID-related quarters and advocating UDC were the most noteworthy. There were two main points in UDC's favour. First, UDC had a strong foothold among many of the specialized information services which might be expected to be early participants in the network. Second, it had lighted on the facet or syntactic dimension in classification long before the appearance of the more explicitly formulated Ranganathanian facet analysis, and could be readily envisaged as being likely to develop systematically and comprehensively in this direction. On the other hand, very drastic changes to UDC would have been necessary to render it serviceable for a global network. If drastic changes in UDC were not made, UDC's delays in updating caused by the procedure that was considered hyperdemocracy would be unacceptable for the scientific information network application.

Following the publication of the *UNISIST Study Report*, an ingenious idea for resolving UDC's difficulties regarding the scientific information network was discussed within FID, and remitted for study to a special Working Group which was set up by the FID/CCC (Central Classification Committee [for UDC]) at its meeting in Warsaw in October 1971. This was the notion of a "Standard Reference Code (SRC)" intended as a "superstructure", which was conceived both as a switching language for the scientific information network, and as an underpinning structure which would direct the way forward to the future development of UDC (Lloyd 1972). However, work on the SRC, which started in January 1972, did not get beyond the production of a list of proposed "superclasses" (FID 1972a), before it was brought to an early end by FID Council. The idea of an independent switching language had prevailed after all. Thus it was UDC's parent body which finally decided that it could not fulfil the switching function in the scientific information network.

The third landmark was the FID SRC Budapest Forum held on 7th September 1972. At the conference papers were nevertheless given on the possibility of using UDC as a switching language (FID 1972b). However, the same conference included another paper which contributed to the clarification of the UNISIST requirement. The paper was presented by Helmut Arntz (FID Vice-President) on behalf of UNESCO (1972). It offered an outline of some of the features of "a broad system of ordering", with some sharpening of the rather general ideas put forward in the *UNISIST Study Report* a year earlier. What had previously been a "world-wide scheme of subject categorizations" became here "a broad classification" of which "... the main function ... is to serve as a switching mechanism to link different individual classifications and thesauri in the process of information transfer". Further, "the BSO should be foreseen as:

(1) a mechanism for shallow indexing, whose goal is to locate and transfer large blocks of information, rather than specific documents or data, between different discipline- and mission-oriented systems, using eventually different ... languages.

(2) a universal scheme embracing all fields of science and technology, with possible extension to other fields of knowledge.

(3) a flexible system keeping pace with the rapid progress in science and technology. It should also be amenable to the application of modern management techniques for revision, updating, and further distribution of revised editions to the users at minimum intervals.

(4) a scheme with simple structure, so that it may be adopted by different information systems without much effort and heavy financial support.

(5) a scheme which could be easily used both by computerized and manual information systems".

Though the paper brought many of the ideas in the *UNISIST Study Report* into clearer focus, it still made no advance in defining what was meant by "broad" or by "large blocks of information". It is interesting to note that "systems" – which presumably may mean both information centres and indexing languages – may be mission-oriented, that is to say, not necessarily of a discipline-oriented character.

3.2 FID/SRC (Subject-field Reference Code) Working Group

Following the FID/SRC Budapest Forum in September 1972, there was a consensus in favour of dissociating the SRC project from UDC revision or reform activities. As a result FID set up a new Working Group "FID/SRC (Subject-field Reference Code)", which was independent both of the FID/ CCC and FID/CR (Study Committee on Classification Research). The new FID/SRC Working Group was charged with designing and developing "a broad subject-ordering scheme", intended to function as below (FID 1973a):

(a) a tool for interconnection of information systems, services and centres using diverse indexing/retrieval languages;

(b) a tool for tagging (i.e. shallow indexing) subject-fields and subfields;

(c) a referral tool for identification and location of all kinds of information sources, centres and services.

With its sphere of activities provisionally marked out as above, the FID/SRC Working Group, with financial support contributed jointly by FID and UNESCO, under contract arrangements, commenced its labours in January 1973. Its eight members, initially drawn from the FID/CCC and FID/ CR, were Jiří Toman as Chairman, Pauline Atherton (later Cochrane), A. Neelameghan, Willem F. de Regt, A.-F. Schmidt, Dušan Simandl, Jan Hendrik de Wijn, together with Geoffrey A. Lloyd, Head of the FID Classification Department as Secretary (later Rapporteur). The first three were members of the FID/CR, recommended by the retiring chairman Rasmus Mølgaard-Hansen. Two additional members were co-opted to the Working Group, of whom Ingetraut Dahlberg had tentatively attended the first meeting held in January 1973 (FID 1973a; FID 1973b), and Eric Coates attended the third meeting held in June 1973 for the first time (FID 1973c).

The FID/SRC Working Group, together with Vladimir Rybatchenkov (UNESCO liaison officer on behalf of UNISIST), met three or four times a year at FID Headquarters in The Hague, with the work of collecting information, listing and drafting being done between meetings by individual members and discussion arising from these activities being carried out by correspondence (UNESCO 1973; Rybatchenkov 1974). After the first year, Atherton (USA) and Neelameghan (India) dropped out because of problems of funding their attendance within the framework of the FID/ UNESCO contract terms.

After the end of 1973, the emphasis of the work turned away from the idea of a provisional classification for control of incoming candidate terms to the establishment of a classification suitable for BSO itself. At the 5th meeting in February 1974 at the FID Secretariat, it was decided to use the name "Subject-field Reference Code (SRC)" for the current project rather than "Broad System of Ordering (BSO)" which was the name hitherto used by UNISIST (FID 1974a).

For a provisional classification, the Working Group made use of the Object Area scheme of Dahlberg (1973). But, at the same time, an alternative classification was prepared, which consciously set out to challenge at every point the assumptions of the Object Area scheme. By the summer of 1974, two proposed classifications for BSO, both of around 1,200 terms, had emerged. Each was supported by about half of the Working Group. The first, Scheme I, was obviously derivative from the provisional Object Area classification used for vocabulary control in 1973. The second, Scheme II, purported to be independent of the provisional Object Area classification. The division of view within the Working Group seemed unfortunate at the time, when it became clear that no resolution would be possible by the date set by UNESCO for evaluation of the project work by independent assessors.

The FID/SRC Working Group by August 1974 had worked through its problem to the extent of producing two schemes, and faced with the need to render an immediate account of itself to the UNESCO assessors, it remained stalled between apparently irreconcilable differences of opinion. If the Working Group had been given sufficient time it is possible that it would have eventually arrived at a unified BSO comprising features taken from both Scheme I and Scheme II. Dahlberg's Object Area scheme and two Schemes are given in outline in *The BSO Manual* (Coates, Lloyd and Simandl 1979a, 16-17, 21-22).

3.3 FID/BSO Panel formed in September 1974

Like the Working Group, the members of the UNESCO panel of four assessors divided evenly in their personal preferences for the respective schemes. However, they thought that the differences between the two schemes were not so great as to be totally irreconcilable, and they recommended that the task of reconciliation should be assigned to a smaller group than the full Working Group (FID 1974b).

At the joint meeting of the full FID/SRC Working Group with UNISIST experts held in The Hague on 11-13 September 1974, the Working Group itself then chose three of its number to carry on the project, now to be called "BSO". Hence the new FID/BSO Panel formed, consisting of Geoffrey Lloyd (Rapporteur), Eric Coates and Dušan Simandl (FID 1975a). The first two had been associated with the compilation of Scheme I, while the third one had been with Scheme II. An unbalance to one side or the other was inevitable there. As from their earlier experience with evenly divided groups in connection with BSO, the sponsoring bodies were reluctant to appoint an even-numbered Panel. Moreover, Scheme I was to a considerable extent faceted, and envisaged unregulated facilities for combining notation to represent composite subjects. The facet element in Scheme II was substantially less than in Scheme I, and no combination facilities were envisaged. The very differences between the two schemes pointed to solutions unlike those offered by either.

The FID/BSO Panel, within six months of its appointment, produced a unified draft (UNESCO 1975), taking into account both Scheme I and Scheme II. As both the parent schemes were incomplete, the number of terms in the unified provisional draft increased to 2,000. The following drafts were prepared by the FID/BSO Panel and submitted for comments (FID 1975b; FID 1977):

March 1975   1st provisional draft, 2,000 terms, without notation (FID/BSO Panel 1975).
This draft was distributed to elicit the comments of some 400 subject and documentation experts, mostly associated with ICSU affiliated bodies; 103 replies were received.

March 1976 1st revised draft, 3,200 terms, notated (FID/ BSO Panel 1976).
This draft was the outcome of consideration of comments received on the 1975 draft. Provided with some rudimentary Time and Place facets, an explicit citation order for composite subjects, and defined restrictions on the kinds of relations to be expressed by combining notations.

August 1977 2nd revised draft, 3,800 terms, with alphabetical index (FID/BSO Panel 1977).
This draft was the result of further study by the BSO Panel, oriented to the need to prepare a scheme to be usable in a field test.

March 1978 3rd revision, 4,000 terms, released (Coates, Lloyd and Simandl 1978b).
This third revised draft, which was also the first published version of BSO, was the result of further amendments found to be necessary after a consideration of results of the field test carried out in the autumn of 1977.

In September 1977, just before the field test, Coates took up the rapporteurship following Lloyd's persuasion. It was Lloyd who invited Coates (1991b) to join the FID/SRC Working Group as a co-opted member in the first half of 1973. Coates gave a good account of himself in the required tasks, which started after the appointment of the new FID/BSO Panel in September 1974 (see Endnote 4). Lloyd (1979) mentioned, "It is largely thanks to Coates's energy and expertise that the raw BSO draft was refined, completed, subjected to a field test in 1977 and finally published in 1978".

4. Concept of a broad ordering system

4.1 Why an ordering system? Ordering system vs. coding system

BSO is not only a subject code but also an ordering system. An ordering system was prescribed because the research projects for an Intermediate Lexicon in Marseilles and in London found it necessary to employ a structured rather than a randomly ordered switching language, and this line of approach was evidently accepted as a valid one. In theory the switching operation requires nothing more than a neutral code system in which concepts are represented. In other words the structure of the neutral code is of no consequence. In practice, however, the main investment of effort in setting up and maintaining such a switching system is in the linking of local indexing concept representations with neutral language representations of the equivalent concepts. This is achieved through the construction of 'equivalence tables' or 'conversion tables' (see Figure 1 above). It is much easier to form these equivalence tables if a neutral language is presented in a systematic form than if the neutral language codes were randomly ordered. Concept representations set forth in systematic order are to a considerable extent self-defining. The risk of mistranslation, and the effort simply of finding the appropriate code are both reduced if the neutral language is in the form of a classification. Each code must represent one concept alone, and each concept must be represented by one code alone. In other words the switching language must be a strictly vocabulary-controlled language. Therefore, the proposed switching language for UNISIST should be a "broad classification".

4.2 Why a broad system? How broad is broad?

The notion of a broad as opposed to a detailed classification in BSO was supported by tactical and economic considerations rather than those relating to inherent technical properties of such a system. A switching language is not set up, maintained and put to daily use without an additional cost. In relation to measurable costs at least, a broad system might seem to hold out a prospect of economic practicability (Coates 1980a).

However, the FID/SRC Working Group which started its labour in January 1973 had considerable difficulties in arriving at an operationally practicable definition of what was to be understood by "broad". The Working Group was on the one hand exhorted not to make the scheme too detailed, and on the other hand not to omit various specialist subject fields, which might well have been left out on certain possible interpretations of "broad". As to the question of "How broad is broad", arithmetical approach (to a total number of terms in advance), hierarchical approach (to some specified hierarchical level), linguistic approach (to qualitative difference between subjects and subject-fields), etc. were discussed, but all these approaches proved fruitless (Coates, Lloyd and Simandl 1979a, 9-11).

The criterion for cut-off adopted finally for what was to be included in the scheme rested upon the extent to which 'organizational activity' and 'institutionalization' were manifested in relation to the 'subject field' or 'area of study'. In other words a subject which had an actual 'organized information source' devoted exclusively to it was to be given its own code in BSO. Organized information source was then further particularized as follows:

*(a) an organization supporting or sponsoring the regular issue of specialist information
*(b) an abstracting and/or indexing service
*(c) an information collection (as a library or data bank)
　(d) a chair of university teaching
　(e) a special subject field periodical

At a later stage of developing BSO, however, it was decided to restrict the scope of 'organized information source', by dropping the categories (d) and (e). A chair of university teaching did not necessarily function as an 'organized information source' in the same manner as organizations in the other four categories. Chairs are sometimes created as a reflection of the eminence of an individual rather than as a token of the existence of an organized field of discourse. The category of special subject periodical was dropped by the BSO Panel, which succeeded the FID/SRC Working Group towards the end of 1974, on account of the impermanence of some specialized periodicals.

The BSO Panel's view is that the content of all the categories of organized information services is subject to change which would need to be monitored by a BSO central bureau, and would subsequently be reflected in changes in the detail level of BSO. However, it seems that changes in periodicals published might present a very expensive and formidable monitoring task which perhaps would not in the end produce very great changes in detail cut-off point as arrived at by consideration of categories (a), (b) and (c).

The criterion for cut-off of detail in BSO was a form of 'institutional warrant'. Documentary or literary warrant, which has been the basis of general classifications, was not used. The use of the criterion for inclusion in BSO has resulted in a compilation of just over 4,000 terms.

5. Structural features of BSO

5.1 Outline of the scheme

The first outline of BSO is presented as Table 1. The notation uses Arabic numerals as the main symbol set. All BSO codes begin with a member of the millesimal array 000 to 999, and these codes are consecutively followed by a member of the centesimal array 00 to 99. Accordingly there is a regular pattern of 3,2,2 ... digits for subject subdivisions in BSO.

The scheme is evidently discipline-oriented, but among the organized information services of which the BSO Panel have taken into account, there are some which are phenomena- or mission-oriented. Accordingly there are some purely phenomena classes such as Human needs (470), Area studies (520) and Social groups and communities (528) in the scheme, and provision is made whereby any phenomenon which is a focus of an 'organized information source' from a multidisciplinary point of view finds an unambiguous place in the system (more will be mentioned in Section 7).

The scheme shows some influence of the 'theory of integrative levels' in the progression of the sciences up from the physical sciences (205), through the life sciences (300), to the social sciences (530). The theory was introduced to the CRG in the late 1950s by Douglas Foskett (1961). The scheme also has similarities to the outline of Henry Bliss' Bibliographic Classification (BC) and the Bliss Bibliographic Classification, 2nd edition (BC2), the principle of which has been recognized as 'gradation by specialities' (Coates 1995a). But the main germinal influence on this aspect of BSO was not Bliss directly but the Object Area scheme of the Ordnungssystem der Wissensgebiete compiled for the DGD by Dahlberg (1973) as mentioned earlier (see Section 3.2). The BSO outline, however, differs from the Object Area scheme of the Ordnungssystem in two main respects. It separates applications of the various physical sciences from their parent sciences, and furthermore it diverges from the Ordnungssystem in separating the technologies associated with Information and Communication from other applications of the physical sciences. Both departures are seen by the compilers of BSO as the best options available within constraints of linear order of knowledge.

Table 1: First outline of BSO

088	Phenomena & entities from a multi- or non-disciplinary point of view	460	Education
		470	Human needs
		475	Household science
SUBJECT FIELDS		477	Work & leisure occupations
100	Knowledge generally	480	Sports & games
112	Philosophy		
116	Science of science	500	Humanities & social studies
118	Logic	510	History & related sciences
120	Mathematics	520	Area studies
125	Statistics & probability	527	Society
128	Computer science	528	Social groups & communities
140	Information sciences	530	Social Sciences
150	Communication sciences	533	Cultural anthropology
160	Systemology & cybernetics	535	Sociology
165	Management	537	Demography
182	Research	540	Political science & politics
186	Testing & trials	550	Public administration
188	Metrology	560	Law
		570	Social welfare
200	Science & technology (together)	580	Economics
		588	Management of enterprises
203	Natural sciences		
205	Physical sciences	600	Technology
210	Physics		
230	Chemistry	910	Language & literature
250	Space & earth sciences		
300	Life sciences	940	Arts
359	Applications of life sciences	943	Plastic arts
360	Agriculture	945	Graphic fine arts
368	Veterinary science	947	Photography as art
370	Forestry	949	Decorative arts & handicrafts
380	Wildlife exploitation	950	Music & performing arts
390	Environment		
410	Biomedical sciences	970	Religion & atheism
445	Behavioural sciences		
450	Psychology	992	Esoteric practices & movements

Apart from 088 Phenomena class which is an empty class prepared for multidisciplinary subjects (as will be mentioned in Section 7), the outline of BSO can best be understood as comprising three sections as follows: (1) Area 112 to 188, a series of methodological sciences and techniques (or collectively the preliminary sciences), applicable to many fields, and necessary tools for activity in the subject fields

200 to 890 (with probable exception of 510 History and 520 Area studies). (2) Area 203 to 588 is in the main a sequence of sciences ranging in ascending order of complexity of the phenomena and entities concerned, beginning with the physical sciences (205), and passing through the life sciences (300) to the social sciences (530) ('integrative levels'). Each science following 210 Physics has methodological and phenomenal aspects which when taken in isolation belong to preceding sciences in the sequence and not to following ones. Conversely each science in the series may contribute 'aspects' to sciences following it, but not to those preceding it. (3) Area 600 to 992 is a sequence of subject fields each of which is centred on humanly generated products of a technological, linguistic, artistic, or spiritual kind.

The whole area 100 to 588 can also be regarded as human mental products. Thus there are four subareas of human products in the BSO outline: (1) 112 to 188, (2) 210 to 588, (3) 600 to 890 (a subject field composed of applications of basic sciences, including physics and chemistry, and subdivided according to the BSO facet pattern to be mentioned in Section 5.2) and (4) 910 to 992. The BSO Panel thought that the underlying pattern of knowledge might be thought of as possessing a cyclic (or possibly spiral) form. Therefore when the first and last subareas are connected, a clockwise cyclic structure of knowledge takes shape as Figure 2. In the cyclic structure the order of (3) (4) (1) is increasing abstraction, and the order of (1) (2) (3) is increasing concreteness. Figure 2 tells us that the problem for classification-maker in converting this cycle into linear form is to cut the cycle in the least unhelpful place. The BSO point of cutting is at the base of the diagram, where philosophy and religion are near each other.

On the issue of the collocation or separation of science and technology, BSO has favoured separation as the lesser of evils. But an exception had been made insofar as agriculture

```
        ┌──────────────────────────────────────────┐
        │                                          ↓
```

480 Sports/games	Humanities/social studies 500
470 Human needs	History/related sciences 510
460 Education	Area studies 520
450 Psychology	Society 527
445 Behavioural sciences	Social sciences 530
420 Medicine	Sociology 535
410 Biomedical sciences	Demography 537
390 Environment	Politics 540
380 Wildlife exploitation	Public administration 550
370 Forestry	Law 560
366 Animal husbandry	Social welfare 570
360 Agriculture	Economics 580
359 Applications of life sciences	Enterprise management 588
340 Zoology	Technology 600
330 Botany	Production technology 620
320 Microbiology	Materials handling 625
310 Biological sciences	Packaging/storage 627
300 Life sciences	Energy technology 631
290 Geography	Materials technology 635
270 Geology	Nuclear technology 640
260 Earth sciences	Electrotechnology 650
250 Space & earth sciences	Thermal engineering 670
230 Chemistry	Mechanical engineering 680
228 Crystallography	Construction technology 710
210 Physics	Environmental technology730
205 Physical sciences	Transport technology 740
203 Natural sciences	Military sci/technology 760
200 Science & technology	Mining 780
188 Metrology	Process industries 800
186 Testing & trials	Metal technology 860
182 Research	Wood/pulp/paper
166 Standardisation	technology 871,95
165 Management	Textiles technology 877
160 Systemology/cybernetics	Particular products
150 Communication sciences	manufacture 890
140 Information sciences	Language/literature 910
120 Mathematics	Arts 940
118 Logic	Religion/atheism 970
112 Philosophy ‖	Esoteric practices 992

Figure 2: BSO & the cycle of knowledge

(360) was collocated with the pure biological sciences (310) and medicine (420) was collocated with human biology (411). The difference was in the level of control: agriculture and

medicine were fostering activities in which in the main vital processes were selectively aided or steered by man, whereas processes in the technologies (600) associated the physical sciences (205) were much more completely controlled by man. For this reason BSO has separated the applications of physics and chemistry (at 600) from the basic sciences, but the life sciences (300) are collocated with their applications, normally at a broad level, but in the case of the biomedical sciences (410) at a more detailed level.

5.2 Facet structures

Within each subject field, the schedule details are arranged in a facet pattern, which is to a considerable extent 'repetitive pattern' or possessing 'structural isomorphism' (Bertalanffy 1968, 80-86) from subject field to subject field with only slight variations as one passes from one major domain to another (e.g. the Natural sciences to the Life sciences, the Life sciences to Human sciences, Human sciences to Technology, Technology to the Mental and Artistic products which follow Technology). The basic facet pattern of BSO is as follows:

(1) Tools or equipment for carrying out operations
(2) Operations (i.e. purposive activities by people)
(3) Processes, interactions
(4) Parts, subsystems of objects of action or study, or of products
(5) Objects of action or study, or products, or total systems

In BSO, 'subject field' is equivalent to 'combination area'. Table 2 shows combination areas in BSO. As will be exemplified in the next section, the table of combination areas is useful for distinguishing between two ways of combining notational elements that constitute a composite subject.

Table 2: Combination areas in BSO

Range	Area	Range	Area
112 to 112, 78, Z	Philosophy	380 to 387, 88	Wildlife exploitation
116 to 116, 70	Science of science	390 to 397, 75, 40	Environment
118 to 118, 55	Logic	410 to 439, 88, 37, 65	Biomedical sciences
120 to 125, 78	Mathematics & statistics	450 to 450, 89	Psychology
128 to 128, 80	Computer science	460 to 467, 76, 30	Education
140 to 148, 78, 32, 79	Information sciences	470 to 478, 80	Human needs
150 to 158, 56	Communication sciences	480 to 489, 60	Sports & games
160 to 170	Systemology, management, standardisation & organisations	510 to 518	History & related sciences
182 to 188, 60	Research, testing, discoveries, inventions, patents & metrology	520 to 529, 79	Area studies & social groups
		530 to 537, 77	Social sciences, cultural anthropology, sociology & demography
210 to 226, 75	Physics	540 to 546, ZW	Political science & politics
228 to 228, 77	Crystallography	550 to 556, 60	Public administration
230 to 238, 30	Chemistry	560 to 568, ZW	Law
252 to 258, 86	Astronomy & space research	570 to 575, 87	Social welfare
262 to 262, 80	Geodesy & surveying	580 to 588, 82	Economics & enterprise management
263 to 268, 87	Geophysics, atmospheric & hydrospheric sciences	600 to 890, 953	Technology
270 to 278, 35, 30	Geology	910 to 928, 70	Language & literature
290 to 295, 65	Geography	940 to 949, 87	Arts
300 to 345, 95	Life sciences	951 to 953, 98, Z	Music
360 to 366, 88, 50	Agriculture, plant & animal husbandry	955 to 957, 70	Performing arts
368 to 368, 63, 50	Veterinary science	970 to 979	Religion & atheism
370 to 370, 92, 65, 70	Forestry	992 to 992, 60	Esoteric practices & movements

In addition to the facet structures embodied in each particular subject field, there are three generally applicable facets: Time, Place and Optional facets. Time (subdivision of -01) and Place (subdivision of -02) common facets are dealt with as in document classification. These are unexceptional, apart from the detail that the ISO 3166 alpha-2 codes (e.g. GB, JP, US, etc.) are used for notation of individual country names. Though these two facets are described as being generally applicable, they are not used in certain cases (notably in the social sciences) where Period and Country are especially provided for in an enumerated schedule.

An Optional facet enabling the type of information source to be specified has been included as a result of the field test carried out in the autumn of 1977. Types of Optional facet are first divided into: Organizations as sources of information (18) and Secondary information sources (20). Next the latter is divided into: Current contents lists (32); Indexes (33); Abstracts (39); and Reviews (40). The facility will also have general practical value in helping indexers to discriminate elements of subject field information from those of type of information source. Details of both kinds frequently appear intermingled. The facet indicator for the Optional facet is shown in notation as two spaces and lack of attention to this factor could cause such an information source title as the British Technology Index (BTI) to be wrongly coded as:

600-026,GB   An information source on the technology (600) of Great Britain (-026,GB)

whereas the correct coding has two spaces between subject field and information source:

600 33-026,GB An index (33), originating in Great Britain (-026,GB), on technology (600)

The Optional facet in BSO is analogous to Form Divisions in

document classifications. It is emphasized in a textbook on subject analysis that care must be taken to distinguish between terms representing subject concepts and terms representing form concepts in the formula of Discipline/ Phenomena/Form (Brown 1982, frames 114 and 128).

6. Syntactic relations and combination facilities

6.1 Internal and external combinations

BSO has comprehensive facilities for combining notational elements to represent composite subjects. Combination of notation for composite subjects raises the issue of citation order, i.e. the order in which notational elements are to be combined. The general instruction is given that within a 'subject field' or 'combination area' (see Table 2), elements of composite subjects are cited in 'reverse schedule sequence'. For example, in 252 Astronomy & astrophysics, the schedule gives:

> 252,28 Satellite astronomy
> 252,72 Sun

The procedure for internal combination is a simple clerical one that links notations in 'reverse schedule sequence' in accordance with the usual 'principle of inversion' in faceted classification. For example, the so-called compound subject "Satellite studies of solar phenomena" is given by citing first the element given later in the schedule (i.e. 252,72 Sun) followed by that given earlier (i.e. 252,28 Satellite astronomy) and deleting the second 252. From the viewpoint of facet pattern described at the beginning of Section 5.2, the cited first element in the above example, namely the concept Sun belongs to facet (5), and the cited second element Satellite astronomy (or Astronomy with satellite) is applicable to facet (2) and (1). But facet (2) has no role in this combination

31

because the operation Astronomy already defines the whole 'combination area'. Facets (3) and (4) are inapplicable to this subject.

The manner in which the two notations thus ordered are linked may be prescribed in the schedule itself by an 'Expand ...' note, or, if there is no prescription, a regular link symbol ,0, is used for combination within the same 'combination area'. In the example in question the notation for "Satellite studies of solar phenomena" is governed by an 'Expand ...' note in the schedule at 252,40 which in effect directs that the two notations 252,72 and 252,28 should be simply placed together, with second 252 deleted, giving 252,72,28. However, if there had been no 'Expand ...' note, the combined notation, which deletes the first digit (2) of the second notation element (252,28) and inserts a regular link symbol (,0,) in the space created, would have been 252,72,0,52,28.

For combinations containing elements drawn from different disciplines, citation order is governed by the following relational formula:

Cite first: the notation for the element denoting application area, mission, purpose, end-product or whole system: more generally the subject which "receives" an action or effect or is seen according to a particular viewpoint, or has a property attributing to it (in short 'recipient').

Cite second: the notation for the element denoting aspect, approach, action applied, agent, or part of a stated whole: more generally the subject element which "contributes" an aspect, approach or action (in short 'aspect contributor').

For example, so-called complex subjects constituted of 450 Psychology and 460 Education are expressed as follows (a hyphen or dash is the external combination device):

450-460 Education in Psychology (or Psychological education)
460-450 Psychology of Education (or Educational psychology)

In the first subject (450-460), Psychology is the 'application area', while Education is the 'action or process applied' to Psychology. In the second (460-450), Education is the 'application area', while Psychology is the 'aspect or approach'. Thus, it is apparent that the question of citation order in the external combination cannot be reduced to the level of a clerical operation as in the internal or intra-field combinations. It is necessary to consider, on the plane of meaning, the relationships between the two elements forming the composite concept.

The schedules of BSO are constructed by considering both facets and relations. Table 3 implies that there are two kinds of relational formula behind two kinds of combination. An external relational formula is described as above. An internal relational formula is concealed behind the facet pattern, but it exists in the schedules themselves as will be exemplified below. Each relational formula is quite general in the sense that it represents a grouping of several different kinds of relations, and it is also deliberately restrictive in its effects in contrast with the colon of UDC, which signifies unspecified relationships. The BSO philosophy is that combination of notation may legitimately be used only for a limited range of commonly occurring relationships. Thus, to the classifier matching concepts and forming combinations according to rule, faceted statements have a rather limited use.

Table 3: Facets and relations in BSO

Combination	Citation order	Roles expressing relationships in composite subjects
Internal	Reverse schedule order must be followed	Implicit roles were used in constructing the schedule: (5) object, product, total system; (4) part, subsystem; (3) process, interaction; (2) operation; (1) tool, equipment.
External	User must decide the role that each concept plays in relation to the other	Roles may be 'Recipient' (i.e. application area, mission, purpose, end-product, whole system) – cited first or 'Aspect contributor' (i.e. aspect, approach, action applied, agent, part) – cited second

Table 4 given on page 36 shows the procedures for combining notation. Below are examples of notation combinations. Each example shows analysis of relationship between two concept elements, which is the smallest unit of relational analysis. Relational analysis as an alternative to categorical view of facets was effectively practised in the British Technology Index under the editorship of Eric Coates (1970b; 1973).

Physics (Application area)   210
Information services (Action applied)   140,60
Information services for physics   210-140,60 (external)

Nuclear reactors (Application area)   642
Economics (Aspect)   580
Nuclear reactor economics   642-580 (external)

Coal mining (Application area)   782,20
Trade unions (Aspect)   580,87
Coal mining trade unions   782,20-580,87 (external)

Sun (Application area)   252,72
Satellite astronomy (Action)   252,28
Satellite astronomy of sun   252,72,28 (internal)
                                         ('Expand ...' note)

Insects (Application area)   345,46
Genetics (Aspect)   340,37
Insect genetics   345,46,0,40,37 (internal)

Chemical plant (Application area)   811,12
Construction technology (Action)   710
Construction of chemical plant   811,12,07,10 (internal)
                                         (area 600 to 890)

Crime (Action)   535,51
Children as social group (Agent)   535,74,32
Juvenile crime   535,74,32,0,35,51 (internal)

Table 4: Procedures for combining notation
(For composite subjects not given in schedules
and not derivable from 'Expand . . . ' notes in schedules)

Internal combinations (Both elements scheduled separately in the same Combination area)		External combinations (Elements scheduled in different Combination areas)
Combination areas other than 600 to 890	Combination area 600 to 890	
1 . Write notations for separate elements in reverse schedule order, side by side, with space for 2 characters between them	1 . Write notations for separate elements in reverse schedule order, side by side, with space for 2 characters between them	1 . Decide combination order according to citation rule (see Table 3)
2 . Delete 1st digit of the 2nd notation element	2 . Insert a comma after the 1st digit of the 2nd notation element	2 . Write down separate notations in chosen combination order
3 . Insert ,0, in the 3 character space created	3 . Insert ,0 in the 2 character space	3 . Insert Hyphen (or Dash) between the 2 notation elements

6.2 Restrictions on the use of combination facilities

There are two restrictions on the use of combination codes in BSO. In deciding whether to use an 'external' combination it is always advisable to check that the composite concept is not a special case of something which is already implied or even explicitly stated in the enumerated schedule. For instance, such an 'organized information source' as "Women in medicine" has been identified. Does the combination of 420

Medicine and 528,43 Woman offer a possible coding answer? The answer depends upon correct elucidation of the relation between two concepts in the instance in question. If the phrase "Women in medicine" means "Women related to Medicine as patients", to use the code 420-528,43 would result in creating ambiguity and disorder, when there is already at schedule location 439 a facet for particular categories of patients. If the phrase means "Women in medical practice", then again the use of 420-528,43 would create disorder, because there is a scheduled caption 420,15 Medical profession, organization and practice. Even though 420,15 has not yet been developed to enable particular categories of practitioners to be specified, it should be chosen as the placing of "Women in medical practice" rather than the combination 420-528,43. However, if the phrase "Women in medicine" covers both of the above possible relationships and possibly other as well, then the use of the combination code would be appropriate. The conclusion is that the following priority order of procedures is advisable:

> Enumerated subdivision, or
> Internal combination, or
> External combination

In connection with the above priority order, the following guidance should be kept in mind:

> Where a composite subject appears to be equally well represented by two or more different second notational elements, the best answer is that which is "the closest in schedule position to the first element" should be chosen. In particular the 'genus-species' relation implied in such phrases as Plastic tube, Dried milk or Pneumatic control systems should not be represented by the combinatory facilities.

There is one further restriction on the use of combination

codes, whether they are of the 'internal' or 'external' type. This is that concept elements which have no specific notation in BSO should not be used in combination codes in which they would appear to be suitable as first cited elements. For example, under the caption of Ethology (318,50), there is:

318,59 Protection *Includes mimicry and coloration

Each of mimicry and protective coloration has a clearly evident place in BSO, but no specific notation. Each shares the notation of 318,59 with Protection as a general topic and with other possible subdivisions of Protection. If such a combination as 318,59-395,60 (Effect of environmental pollution on protection) were used also for "Effect of environmental pollution on mimicry" or for "Effect of environmental pollution on protective coloration", this would result in the intrusion of the restricted subjects "mimicry" and "coloration" into the otherwise homogeneous block of material, notated 318,59-, on various aspects of protection as a whole. A useful guidance is that better order is kept if such a use of merely 'included' subjects in combination is prohibited.

As to the above restriction, a more useful advice is given by the BSO Panel. It is suggested to add a further "digit or symbol" to the notation when it is applied to the 'included' subjects. By this means the material on Mimicry and Protective coloration can be sorted out from that on Protection, though the two 'included' subjects will still be together an alien body embedded in material on 'equal' subject Protection. It is suggested that the distinguishing digit might be a single terminal comma for the 'included' subjects. This would cause an 'included' subject to sort between the external combination of the 'equal' subject and its internal combinations. This is not an ideal position, but there can be no ideal position short of developing the schedule to more detail. The effect of this measure would be as follows:

318,50   Ethology
318,59   Protection
318,59-   Protection (External combinations)
318,59,   Mimicry
318,59,   Protective coloration
318,59,0, Protection (Internal combinations)
318,59,10 to ,99 (Possible future expansion under
          Protection)

7. Multidisciplinary subjects

Material about objects and phenomena considered from a multi-aspect point of view has long been a problem in document classifications based primarily on knowledge breakdown by disciplines. BSO is also of this kind, and the problem can also arise in subject indexing at the level of 'institutional warrant'. For this reason provision is made for coding this material at 088 (see Table 1) in cases where there is not a predominantly discipline-oriented point of view. However, it is one thing to find a place for multidisciplinary subjects, but another to find a mechanism for individualizing every separate entity or phenomenon which might require this treatment by the classification. BSO uses the principle of 'unique definition' or 'uniquely definable class', which was first suggested in the 1950s as an answer to this problem by Jason Farradane (CRG 1961), and is also recognizable as a mechanism in the Bliss Bibliographic Classification, 2nd edition (BC2).

Most phenomena and entities are uniquely defined in terms comprehended by a particular discipline. For example, the class of entities "Insects" is uniquely defined in zoological terms, not in terms of systems of invertebrate exploitation, nor in terms of the properties by which insects may be pests, nor in terms of their role in mythology. Individualization is achieved by adding to 088 the BSO number for the entity or phenomenon as found in the class within which it is uniquely defined. Thus insects (all aspects) is coded in BSO as 088 (Entities and phenomena from a multidisciplinary point of view) followed by 345,46 (Insects in the discipline within which they are uniquely defined, i.e. Zoology) giving the combined notation 088,345,46. Thus Insects receive different treatments as follows:

088,345,46   INSECTS, All or many aspects

345,46   INSECTS, Zoological aspects only

It should be noted that there are three insertions of non-disciplinary material in the main sequence of subject fields (see Table 1). One enumerated entity/phenomena-based class is 470 Human needs, covering Food (all aspects), Clothing (all aspects), Housing (all aspects) and Leisure (all aspects). These topics, associated with the basic activities of daily life, do not satisfactorily fit into any framework of disciplines (CRG 1978). The second class is 520 Area studies which are multi-disciplinary in character. The third class is 528 Social groups and communities, such as Women (all aspects as discussed in Section 6.2), Racial Minorities (all aspects), the Aged (all aspects) and the Disabled (all aspects). The first and third entities and phenomena straddle both the Human sciences and Technology and often parts of the Life sciences and Natural sciences as well. Accordingly material which could be placed at 470 to 489 (Human needs), at 520 (Area studies) or at 528 to 529 (Social groups and communities) should not be placed at 088. These three non-disciplinary areas have been included in BSO on the basis of identified 'institutional warrant'.

Besides 088 Phenomena class, there is another "empty class" provided in BSO. It is class 890 (Manufacture and technology of particular products not scheduled in the fields 600 to 878), where a similar mechanism is applied to the problem of individualizing technical products. Below are examples of some subjects classified at 890:

890,150,42	Stationery (or writing material) manufacture
890,200,73	Electron microscopy manufacture
890,230	Chemical laboratory equipment manufacture
890,420,22	Medical instruments manufacture
890,472	Clothing & adornment articles manufacture
890,953	Musical instruments manufacture

In BSO products defined by purpose or designed for a particular purpose are classified at the end of the Technology schedule at 890 and individualized by reference to the BSO code for the particular purpose, elsewhere in the scheme. It is necessary to emphasize "elsewhere in the scheme" as the purpose of some products is simply to contribute to more complex technology. Such products (e.g. Switchgear) with a role internal to technology are normally enumerated in the BSO technology schedules. The scheduled heading covers both their manufacture and use (Manufacture can be distinguished from use by employment of the suffix ,06,20 taken from 620 Production technology). One consequence of the policy for individualizing those products with purposes external to technology is that 877,60 Cloth and fabric technology does not schedule manufacture of clothing as a product. The technology of the purpose-defined product Clothing is classified at 890,472. The 472 is taken from the Human needs code for clothing.

8. Notation

The notation of BSO is intended to be read by human users. There are good reasons why a notation intended to be read and stored in a computer might be different. The humanly read notation is under constraints on matters of length and complexity which do not seriously trouble the machine, because all species of digits are in any case converted to numerical values, and a superficially mixed notation has no terrors for it. The BSO notation is believed to be tolerably brief. Over 90% of the uncompounded terms cited in the schedules have codes of 5 numerical symbols length. Arabic numerals are used as the main symbol set, and other symbols are used only very sparingly.

The BSO notation has been devised particularly with the question of updating in mind. The notation does no more than mechanize the order and gives no structural information as to hierarchy. As Coates (1957) has demonstrated there is a mutual constraint between notational expressiveness and hospitality. When a classification scheme employs hierarchically non-expressive notation it is able to admit new subjects, without limit, at their logically correct positions. The BSO has to some extent sacrificed brevity by leaving large unused notational gaps for future use. These gaps will often facilitate updating, though are not absolutely essential to it, and the system will not be frozen when they are all filled.

The notation uses Arabic numerals, plus semantically empty punctuation symbols (comma and hyphen/dash) which however have an assigned ordinal value lower (i.e. higher in a list written from top to bottom) than the series 0 to 9. The Roman alphabet A to Z ordering is occasionally used for listing of individual entities (e.g. 940,A to ,Z Individual artists). Some notation elements are drawn from outside the coding system, such as the ISO 3166 alpha-2 codes for names of countries, and the groups of the Periodic table also employ Roman numerals. The use of characters supplementary to numerals demands a fixed system of ordinal values. The following sequence gives the 'ordinal value' system for files organized by BSO:

Spaces after last symbol of notation

Two spaces followed by further numerical characters

(This occurs when the Optional facet for type of source is used)

- followed by further numerical characters
(The hyphen is the connecting symbol for external combination of notation)

, followed by further characters
(The comma is a semantically empty symbol which introduces intercalated numbers filing between consecutive members of a notational array)

00 to 99 or 000 to 999
(These two sets never occur together in a file in such a way as to require ordinal preference between them)

A to Z
(These are used when individualization rather than grouping is required at the end of each notation)

All codes begin with a member of the millesimal array 000 to 999. Between any two subjects represented by consecutive members of the millesimal array, further subjects may be interposed by adding to the first of the two consecutive millesimal numbers a comma followed by a two-digit code belonging to the centesimal array 00 to 99. In similar manner further subjects may be interposed between consecutive members of the 00 to 99 array by adding a comma followed by two digits from a further 00 to 99 array. As a result there is a regular pattern of 3,2,2, ... digits (e.g. 911,15,50 Linguistics > Translation > Machine translation). But this pattern is varied when notational combinations occur, in view of the fact that the combinations include link symbols (- or ,0,). The numbers 088 and 890 are the leading number groups of untypical pattern of 3,3,2,2, ... digits.

The 'filing order', including the 'ordinal value' of spaces, numerals, symbols and letters used in the BSO notation, is as follows:

000	A Subject
000 18 to	
000 40	Optional facet for type of information source
000-01	Time facet
000-02	Place facet
000-100 to	
000-992	External combination with another subject in another 'Combination area'
000,0,	Internal combination with another subject within the same 'Combination area'
000,09, to	
000,99	Enumerated subdivision of the subject, or, the next following cognate subject

Within a 'Combination area', the 'combination order' or 'citation order', is the reverse of the above 'filing order' in accordance with the 'principle of inversion'. Accordingly a usual combination order in BSO is as follows:

Enumerated subdivision, or)
Internal combination, or   ) /Place/Time/Optional facet
External combination   )

However, there are occasions when the Place or Time property refers only to the first element in a combination. In this case the Place or Time notation should immediately follow that of the element to which the particular Time or Place refers (e.g. 786-026,RU-580,62,40 Imports of Russian oil and gas).

It is stated early in this section that the present notation is intended for the human user. This is not to say that it is intended only for manual switching systems. Computer processed switching systems also have human users of switching languages at both input and output ends of the switching system. Also it is not to say that the notation could not be fed to a computer for switching between symbols having the same meaning in different local indexing languages. However, the BSO Panel thought that if facilities for combining switching with interactive computer-aided search were required, it would be preferable to employ another notation containing built-in cues enabling the machine to traverse requested search paths.

Finally the structure of the scheme is in no way dependent upon the notation. The present notation could be uncoupled and a different notation could be attached without affecting the essential character of the system. The only proviso is that any new notation should have no less versatility than the present one in its ability to handle combination and to produce the required order.

9. System design and priority

It has been suggested that a switching indexing language needs to be economical in usage. The benefits of networking are not obtainable entirely without cost. The indexing of material by a switching language at a centre would be an addition to indexing effort normally put forth for local purposes. It is essential that the additional cost of communication with other centres in the network should not contain any unnecessary element. A classification user's unnecessary costs arise mainly in two ways. First, day-to-day application of the scheme may demand more decision effort than is necessary. Second, the local implementation of update amendments to the scheme may involve unnecessary effort.

Unnecessary decision effort is the result either of gross

mismatch between the subjects found in the material to which the classification is to be applied and the concepts represented in the classification itself, or to lack of structural homogeneity in the scheme itself. Mismatch is the result not only of initial shortcomings of the scheme but also of delays in updating. Lack of structural homogeneity may be paraphrased as unnecessary complexity in the scheme due to absence of an overall pattern. An example of an inhomogeneous general classification would be one which was prepared simply by bringing together the special classifications corresponding to each included subject area, and listing them sequentially (possibly in some helpful order). According to Coates (1995a), a typical instance of this kind is the Library of Congress Classification (LCC) which is based on literary warrant of the holdings of LC. Any discipline represents a particular viewpoint. A series of classifications, each optimal for the needs of a particular viewpoint, form a general classification of great complexity, and consequently demand excessive decision effort in being applied.

Unnecessary effort in implementing updating, both on the part of the updater and of the user, is demanded when the insertion of a new subject requires not only an addition to the schedule but also a re-notation of adjacent terms representing old knowledge. This may arise either because the area involved was in the first place inadequately structured or because of a constraint offered by the notation.

These considerations are reflected in the general features of BSO, which include a marked incidence of structured pattern, both within and transcending discipline boundaries. The system is also highly prescriptive. There are no alternative placings offered. Completely definitive and embracing procedures are laid down by which indexers deal with the necessary factor of cross-classification in the schedule, which is therefore expected to be non-ambiguous in use and predictable in updating.

The *UNISIST Study Report* of 1971, in considering whether any existing classification could assume the functions of the required switching language, stressed the question of management and maintenance. At that time the established general classifications for library purposes appeared to suffer from the matter of updating. A policy of minimal change brings these classifications under criticism for being unable to handle contemporary knowledge. The contrary policy of change at intervals to incorporate changes in knowledge involves users in the costs of making amendments to records, which may be retrospective in effect. These costs are frequently too heavy to be borne.

The above lesson has been noted by those concerned with the development of BSO, and the view has been formed that the cost and effort of management, and particularly of updating, is in many respects a function of the technical features of a system. An attempt has been made to design BSO so as to minimize the likely cost of updating both to system revisers, and perhaps even more importantly, to users. It is perhaps the emphasis upon this factor as a priority which most distinguishes BSO from other general classifications already established in the field.

This priority is given effect by contributions from three features of BSO: (1) the scheme is pervasively analytico-synthetic, i.e. terms may be combined notationally to represent the limited number of syntactic relationships likely to be needed at a broad 'institutional warrant' level; (2) there is a considerable element of 'structural isomorphism' in the manner in which each discipline is broken down; and (3) the function of the notation is limited to mechanizing the order as mentioned in the previous section. Each of these factors contributes to ease of updating.

10. Testing and possible applications of BSO

10.1 Three test exercises

As has been mentioned, three major test exercises were undertaken in 1977, 1981 and 1982/3 respectively. All of these exercises were carried out by the FID/BSO Panel with the financial support of FID and UNESCO.

The first tested the usability of BSO by classifiers without prior knowledge of the scheme, and without benefit of a familiarization process. Using the BSO 2nd revised draft with 3,800 terms, and taking the occasion to prepare a subject index to the schedules (FID/BSO Panel 1977), 28 testers located at 26 institutions in 11 countries (Canada, Czechoslovakia, France, India, Japan, Norway, Poland, Soviet Union, United Kingdom, United States and West Germany) were selected. Each tester assigned BSO codes to test samples totalling 150 items of data taken from data comprising directory entries relating to databases, abstracting and indexing services and international organizations, which amounted to 850 items in all. The results of the test were moderately encouraging. A mean agreement of 43% with the Panel's control answers was achieved. The highest individual score was 60% and the lowest 31%. The BSO Panel drew the conclusion from these figures that when the lessons of the test had been incorporated into BSO, which had included the Optional facet for the type of information source, and users had been introduced to the scheme through a full familiarization programme, then one would expect in real life that the mean figure for agreement in applying the scheme might be around 70%. The FID/BSO Panel (Coates, Lloyd and Simandl 1979a, 32-33) felt that this would be an acceptable basis for switching. The schedules and index, modified as the result of the test, became the first published version of BSO which appeared in 1978.

The second, i.e. the BSO Switching Test of 1981, was a straightforward exercise in index switching between two specialist centres with a certain amount of common subject overlap in marginal-interest areas (FID 1980). The test compared the results of direct switching between the two local indexing languages, and BSO-mediated switching between them. The core subject area of the two centres were Ferrous metallurgy and Welding respectively. One centre used UDC as the indexing language, and the other used a specialist thesaurus in the field of Welding. The results of the switching test showed that there was no great difficulty in switching between two local indexing languages of different kinds, but that there were considerable problems in switching from an exhaustively applied post-coordinate indexing language to the pre-coordinate indexing language of UDC. These were in part resolved by modification of the Grouping Sections of the thesaurus. The results also showed that the mediating language performed best when used for switching material of interest to both parties in the switching transaction, but that even in these areas BSO was often not specific enough to switch in a manner adequate to meet the need of the recipient centre. There were fairly marked directional effects in the effectiveness of the switching. These were attributable both to the size of the output language relative to that of the input language, and to the incidence of structural ambiguity in the output language (Coates, Lloyd and Simandl 1981d).

The third, i.e. the BSO Referral Test of 1982/83, was derived from a joint paper by Brian Vickery and Ia McIlwaine (1979) that was included in a special issue devoted to BSO (The rest of papers were: Coates 1979b; Foskett 1979; Perreault 1979; and Soergel 1979. For reply to critics, see Coates 1981b). Following a meeting between Eric Coates and Brian Vickery in London in the spring of 1980, a plan for the field test was drawn up by the BSO Panel. The test was carried out at the University of London Central Information Service (LUCIS) headed by Alina Vickery. The test investigated the effect on retrieval, during the referral step of online searches, of the use of an index to 36 databases frequently searched in the DIALOG host system. The index was prepared by converting each database's 'category codes' or 'grouping terms' to a common form via BSO. The results suggested that while the BSO-based index would not effectively substitute for the dialogue between intermediaries and enquirers and for the dialogue between intermediaries and the machine system, its effects were that more databases were consulted than in conventional referral, and that the level of performance over a set of requests is less variable when such a lexical tool is used in referral. It was not possible to test the effect of using both conventional dialogue and the index by direct comparison in the referral step, but it seemed that in many circumstances the combination would enhance ultimate performance. About 23% of the 'category codes' and 'grouping terms' of the 36 databases chosen could not be converted to BSO index form because there was no corresponding specific BSO notation to match them, and this handicap needs to be kept in mind in assessing the likely value of similar but adequately specific universal lexical aids in referral. An expanded version of the *BSO Referral Index* used in the test was published (Coates et al. 1985a). Either version was produced on the computer of the European University Institute in Florence, Italy (Coates et al. 1985b).

It should be added that a project for an Expert System for Referral started at LUCIS in 1984, with Alina Vickery as project leader and with a grant from the British Library Research and Development Department for 20 months. The aim of the project was to develop a microcomputer program named PLEXUS that would aid the searcher to identify the most appropriate reference books to answer a query in the field of gardening/horticulture. The program used artificial intelligence (AI) techniques to structure the interaction between searcher and database (FID 1984a). As a result of the BSO Referral Test the LUCIS researchers were confident enough to decide that a portion of the BSO schedule should be employed as the knowledge base in PLEXUS (Vickery et al. 1986; Vickery et al. 1988).

10.2 Ten distinct categories of possible BSO applications

During the two test exercises in the first half of the 1980s, the FID/BSO Panel examined possible applications of BSO (Coates 1980b; International Classification 1980; FID 1985), and a publicity leaflet for BSO was issued by FID (1984b), in which nine distinct categories of BSO applications were presented. Below are those categories which the BSO Panel recognized, each of which is followed by a known operational instance except the second one. Of course other applications of BSO may have already been carried out into effect without being reported.

1. Overview of knowledge
   • *Enciclopedia della Scienza e della Technica*. Milano: Mondadori, 1976.
2. Subject indication quasi-standard, directory codes, codes for disseminated reports, trade literature
3. Aid to compiling information languages (i.e. indexing languages)
   • *JICST Classification Table*. Tokyo: Japan Information Center of Science and Technology, 1981, succeeded by 2nd 1987 and 3rd 1993 editions. JICST was a semi-national institution sometimes compared with Russian VINITI (All-Union (later All-Russian) Institute for Scientific and Technical Information) and/or French CNRS.
4. Medium for switching between information languages
   • A combination of MISON Rubricator and BSO was in use in Poland.
   MISON was a Russian acronym standing for International Social Sciences Information System

(Soviet Union and later Russia).
5. Referral tool for online terminals
   • *BSO Referral Index: A Subject Index to 36 Data-Bases in the DIALOG System.* Published by the FID/BSO Panel, 1985. (FID publication, 634).
6. Adjunct subject code for files using computer title-word search for in-depth subject retrieval
   • *Bibliography of the Works of Scientific Workers of SR Croatia (BRZR).*
   Machine-readable file maintained at the National and University Library in Zagreb.
7. Sole subject code for information file
   • FID/ET (Study Committee on Education and Training) Clearinghouse collection.
8. Knowledge base for expert systems research
   • PLEXUS: an Expert System for Referral developed by LUCIS, UK.
9. Teaching model for classification studies in schools of library and information science
   • Emporia State University, School of Library Science, Kansas, USA.

While the author was putting together this article, another category of possible BSO applications was recognized, which would be regarded as the tenth one as follows:

10. Information language as a search aid in retrieval and as a teaching aid in general education

The above category is, as it were, the ultimate usage of an indexing language, because it could be used by end users as well as classifiers. This means that the acquisition of an information language and an understanding of classification will improve each user's effectiveness in retrieval in the age of an information-skilled society, where ability to come to terms with, and to navigate through, the diversity of knowledge fields would be an essential part of the required skills (Coates 1997a; Kawamura 2018, section 6).

10.3 How to cope with lack of specificity

It has been mentioned in the introduction that in form BSO was a non-explicitly faceted classification. The non-explicitly or implicitly faceted classification of BSO is partly due to the criterion of 'institutional warrant', i.e. facets may be empty or contain only one or two terms, and is partly due to the BSO's unusual stance on facets. In relation to the latter Coates (1979b) argued, "It is, in fact, a faceted system, though it has not been thought advantageous to set out the facet structure explicitly and in a formal manner in the schedules". Also, Coates (1981b) explained, "To the classifier matching concepts and forming combinations according to rule, facet statements have a rather limited use. ... it is not requisite to have this knowledge in order to be able to classify by BSO".

At the BSO Open Meeting in Lyngby, Denmark in August 1980 (International Classification 1980), which was held on the occasion of the 40th FID Conference and Congress in Copenhagen, Coates (1980b) mentioned that if use of BSO required at every stage much more specificity than BSO offered, then BSO must be ruled out. Therefore, the question arises, "Could BSO be further expanded so as to be usable for classification of documents?" The FID/BSO Panel (Coates, Lloyd and Simandl 1978b, iii) has already answered that there was no practical nor technical reason which would bar such expansion. But it is always true that there exists the time lag between lack of specificity and official updating by a central bureau. In this respect advice given by Coates (1980b) is helpful, "... even here there may be occasions when the further elaborating and detailing of BSO schedules by users themselves may be the most economical way of carrying out the task".

To cope with BSO's lack of specificity, a tentative remedy

was implied at the end of Section 6. The suggested remedy was called 'verbal features' and would be exemplified as follows:

318,59
318,59-
318,59,Mimicry
318,59,Protective coloration
318,59,0,

This kind of remedy had been practised as 'verbal extensions' during the early twenty-years (1951-70) of the British National Bibliography (BNB, 1950-) under the leadership of Eric Coates, the then Chief Subject Cataloguer. BNB employed the Dewey Decimal Classification (DDC), but the scheme matched up neither to the specificity required even at book level, nor to the need for a consistently ordered display of classified material. To mitigate this problem BNB adopted Ranganathan's method of facet analysis using the PMEST formula. The superimposition of the facet formula on a non-faceted scheme of DDC was carried out without notation. For the insertion of 'verbal extensions', BNB devised the symbol [1], the 'ordinal value' of which was between 0 and 1, and additional faceted terms followed the symbol (Wells 1957). In the case of BSO semantically empty punctuation symbols, i.e. comma and hyphen/dash, each of which has an assigned 'ordinal value' and is positioned in the prescribed 'filing order', play an important role in adopting 'verbal features'.

It must be added that an accumulation of faceted extensions was published by BNB (1963), and that the publication became a useful guide to an official revision of DDC. In connection with BSO, Coates (1980a) envisaged a new method of updating, where an updating decision would be a matter of application of agreed rules by a central bureau, with the participation of users, rather than a search by an expert committee for a consensus (which may not exist) or for a collective intuition. This plan was based on his belief, "If the initial scheme is sufficiently structured according to underlying principles which can be communicated, then updating decisions can be swift and the task of the bureau itself". In short the answer is in the BSO schedules themselves. Coates (1980b) expressed himself paradoxically, "I am in favour of a revolution, not of classifications, but of the management of classifications".

11. Decline of classification

This section was added following a proposal made by one of three anonymous referees. BSO has not been updated in the 28 years since 1994. As a broad classification the BSO's delay in updating might not be such a serious problem as for other established general classifications, but updating will be needed if it is to be used now. BSO is unknown to many people even in the field of knowledge organization (KO), and the majority of those who know of BSO believe that it has not been actually used but mostly used for demonstration purposes. To borrow the referee's words, like most faceted classifications BSO is not a success story. How should we understand this reality, including the reception of BSO?

11.1 Reception of BSO

Almost all judgements on the 1978 BSO have been expressed by 1982; these were reviewed by Hazel Madeley (1983) of Australia. As might be expected, the 1978 BSO had a mixed reception. Vickery and McIlwaine (1979) gave a very favourable view as below:

"Since it possesses a logical structure and a modern approach to the ordering of knowledge it could appeal as an international bibliographic standard for a systematic arrangement. Its comparatively broad specification and

55

rigid citation order would be an advantage in such a situation, and its lack of flexibility in this respect, in contrast with a scheme like UDC, would be an asset for standardisation, which discourages individual variations in approach".

Alasdair Kemp (1979) in his book review recommended BSO to be utilized as below because it had considerable potential beyond its original purpose:

"Anyone looking for a modern, useful, general classification of knowledge, for whatever purpose, will do well to begin by an examination of BSO".

Jean Perreault (1979), following critical analysis of BSO as to various aspects of the scheme, ranked it tentatively in his "a graph of classificatory perfection" as below. A sudden reference to CC (Colon Classification) was due to his thought that CC was "the only really theoretically viable universal classification". To conclude, he suggested comparisons of BSO, UDC and DDC regarding the aspects that he had pointed out.

(perfect) –

    CC
    BSO/UDC/DC
    LC
(useless) –

The most unfavourable judgement was made by Dagobert Soergel (1979). He was the strongest critic of BSO and concluded that:

"… an abridged version of UDC or of DDC have done at least as well, or rather as badly, as this scheme for the purposes to be served by BSO".

The above two Americans almost ignored the theoretical development of general classification embodied in BSO. From a historical viewpoint Hans Wellisch (1979), another American, argued that the following two factors were likely to doom to failure the European effort towards using a common language:

(1) The longstanding and ingrained aversion of American librarians and information specialists to classification schemes as retrieval tools, and the bulk of information services is now being produced and disseminated in the USA.

(2) It is institutional or organizational backing rather than intrinsic merit which determines whether a general classification scheme survives.

As to the first problem Ranganathan (1955) had disclosed Bliss' grief:

"There was a touch of pessimism in his letters to me. He often referred to the apathy, and even antagonism, on the part of some in his homeland, to the scholarly work on which he had turned his whole life".

The second argument meant that only DDC, UDC and LCC have survived, not so much because they were better than any of the others, such as Cutter's Expansive Classification (EC), Bliss' Bibliographic Classification (BC), Rider's International Classification (RIC), and so on. On behalf of the BSO Panel, Coates (1981b) critically commented on Wellisch's argument as follows:

"The Panel accepts that a scheme weak in organisational support, though strong in merit, has a low survival probability. It is, however, necessary to beware of the converse of this proposition. Whatever may have been the case in the past, it does not follow that a general classification devised at the present time, which is strong on organisational support but weak on merit, would survive. On the contrary, the continuing survival of older, institutionally well-supported schemes of dubious technical merit would ensure its early demise".

There could be a rejoinder to the above comment, i.e. DDC, UDC and LCC still survive, for the time being at least. But Vickery and McIlwaine (1979) have pointed out, "The Decimal Classification has survived over a hundred years although one could argue that it has not survived unscathed". Moreover, following a close examination of BSO, Antony Foskett (1979) confessed, "At one time, I might have advocated spending the money allocated to the development of the BSO on a major attempt to rescue UDC from the morass into which it has slowly been descending in recent years. I am now reluctantly convinced that to do so would have been a fruitless exercise ... The BSO must not be allowed to fall the same trap of amateurism and 'hyperdemocracy', to use Lloyd's own word".

Coates (1980b) came to the conclusion that there were three factors determining whether or not BSO would or would not be used in a given situation: (1) whether existing classifications would do the job as an ordering system; (2) whether the problem of lack of specificity could be resolved (as has been discussed in Section 10.3); and (3) whether BSO was going to continue, with the sufficient resources to ensure continuity.

11.2 Is there a substitute for BSO?

A strong critic of BSO was also in Europe. In 1980 the UNESCO Division for the International Development of the Social Sciences decided to launch a project for the establishment of an integrated social science thesaurus

(Litoukhin 1982). The preparatory work included: (1) a comparative analysis of the available documentary languages by J. Meyriat; (2) a study of the applicability of BSO to provide the structural framework for such an integrated system by I. Dahlberg (1980); (3) a study of the compatibility of BSO, UDC and the MISON Rubricator sponsored by the Working Group 3 of the European Cooperation in Social Science Information and Documentation (ECSSID WG3) by M. Palnicov (1982); and (4) a compilation of the bibliography of mono- and multi-lingual vocabularies and thesauri by M. Krommer-Benz.

The result of above (2) was frightful. Dahlberg concluded: (a) BSO's coverage of the social sciences was found to be relatively small compared with the corresponding classes of DDC, BC2 and the UNESCO Thesaurus; (b) BSO fell short in its structural features as exemplified by its method of class formation and concept arrangement with its reversing rule for citation order; (c) BSO was not designed for the purpose of integrating other systems; and therefore (d) It could not be blamed for its non-suitability for such an application. As the first outline of BSO (see Table 1) implied, the interpretation of social sciences is variable in contrast with that of technology which is applications of basic sciences. For example, the social sciences in DDC included statistics, in BC2 they included religion and history, and in the UNESCO Thesaurus they included psychology and human environment. Dahlberg criticised nearly all aspects of BSO. Coates (1981c) strongly disagreed.

Dahlberg's criticism against BSO was deep-rooted. In view of the era of the Internet, Dahlberg (1996) suggested that the ISKO should support setting up a switching system of library catalogues. Six general classifications selected were: DDC, UDC, LCC, CC, BC2 and the Russian LBC (Library-Bibliographical Classification). The language she proposed for switching between these was the Information Coding

Classification (ICC) developed by herself in 1982. Dahlberg rejected BSO for the reason that BSO embodied neither the 'theory of integrative levels' nor 'facet structure'. Moreover, she criticised BSO for its centesimal notation (3,2,2, ...). She insisted that the human mind usually could not keep in its memory more than nine digits at one time. While BSO incorporated many features drawn from post-1945 classification theory, ICC still divided knowledge into ninefold (9 x 9) divisions, which seemed to fit decimal notation. Coates did not refer to ICC at all, but it is doubtful whether Dahlberg's ICC could stand up to close criticism such as Coates (1981b) received for BSO.

Jacques Maniez (1997) was another strong critic of BSO in Europe. To carry out theoretical research on the compatibility of indexing or information languages, he relied on the lessons of linguistics and development of automatic translation. He proposed two types of viable solutions: the harmonization of several indexing languages (difficult and expensive); and the automatic harmonization of indexing formula(s) [i.e. the combination of one or more indexing terms attached to a document, or used to express a query] through pre-established concordance tables (easier but hampered by structural discrepancies).

In the later part of the paper he referred to the idea of using BSO as a switching or mediating language. He said, "This model is so fascinating that a project was launched in the 70s by UNISIST. ... But we must admit that the results of the study were never encouraging". Though promising results had been obtained from research projects on Intermediate Lexicon (see Section 2), he rejected the model with only thirteen words as above without any reference to a project report.

Maniez argued that "bidirectional convertibility" between information languages would not be possible because of their irreconcilable structures, and that this meant that a project for a universal switching language was doomed to failure. However, his discussion considered only the problem of direct compatibility between two indexing languages, inferred from the case of natural language, and did not consider the use of a switching or mediating language designed to play a role of harmonization between indexing languages despite their structural discrepancies.

There is still a fundamental fallacy in Maniez's argument, because he believed that controlled languages tend to promote internal consistency within information systems while paradoxically reducing intersystem compatibility, so that natural language systems are inherently more compatible than those using controlled languages. Two important matters are overlooked. First, concept representations set forth in systematic order are to a considerable extent self-defining (see Section 4.1) so that the compatibility of two classifications mediated by BSO is expected to result in rather good performance. Second, a natural language system cannot effectively participate in networking because of the lack of clear definitions of the concepts which it represents.

In Maniez's theoretical system the most awkward case was the compatibility of two classifications, and the easiest one was that of two thesauri. Thus what was required there was simply that "... the construction of a concordance table between languages of the same kind", which "can to some extent be computer-aided via a program that detects identical forms in the indexes of classifications and identical or equivalent terms in thesauri". As a result the remaining problem to be solved was switching from classification to thesaurus and vice versa. The proposed remedy was decomposition of pre-coordinate indexing formulas while using the "bilateral and unidirectional" concordance tables.

In the early part of his paper Maniez mentioned, "... the

compatibility of language is not an intrinsic quality but rather a target to be reached". It is evident that Maniez applied a lower level quality to his system than BSO, particularly that he entirely eliminated the syntactic structures from his system saying that "But taking syntactic structures into account in indexing formula would require sophisticated and expensive programs similar to automatic translation software, for a worthless result". Thus he kept readers away from the superior structure of BSO. The conclusion was that "While I. Dahlberg attributes this failure [i.e. not being used as an intermediate language] to the poor structure of the BSO classification, we think that the reason is rather to be found in the inadequacy of the theoretical approach". Dahlberg did not give such an expression as "poor structure".

Strange to say, Maniez scarcely considered the problem in 'concept matching' and 'vocabulary control'. Robert Fugmann (2004), another practical researcher in information field and real thinker as Coates was, asserted that the linguistically based definition of 'concept' was inadequate. He explained:

"Concept, as the core entity in the information field, is currently widely understood as the meaning of a word, a view that has been adopted from linguistics. But in the information field we must recognize a concept entirely independent of whether or not it happens to have been assigned a lexical expression in natural or technical language. In other words, in our view a concept exists independent of whether natural language has (already) coined for it a lexical unit. In its initial stage of emergence a concept must even be presented in the nonlexical, paraphrasing mode of expression. Many concepts never become lexicalized in natural language and only in classifications through the notations assigned to them".

Likewise, in his teaching on classification, Ranganathan

(1967, 327-328) showed the well-known three-plane model: (1) the idea plane, (2) the verbal plane, and (3) the notational plane. Later in view of the era of computerized information retrieval, Coates (1988a) restructured the three-plane model as: (1) the concept plane and (2) the symbol plane (the verbal plane, the notational plane, and so on). Using the reduced two-plane model, Coates detailed:

"Computers operate entirely on the symbol plane. They can accept, manipulate, process, and give out symbols. They cannot move to plane 1 – the idea plane. ... One cannot operate on the idea plane, one cannot analyse, separate, compare, one cannot think without calling up natural language in aid. ... An information language is not primarily a list of terms, but rather a list of concepts, each one of necessarily to be labelled with a term, that is to say with a symbol. It is here that the idea of vocabulary control arises. It is the symbol, the label, word or phrase which has to be controlled, not the concept itself, and the target of the control is to try ensure that each concept is uniquely labelled with one symbol alone and that a given symbol labels only one concept".

According to Coates, classification has the advantage that "There is a one-to-one correlation between concept and symbol in classification". This proposition produced another important one: "Classification is or should be the basis of information languages", which can be paraphrased as "Classification as the basis for non-classificatory-form information languages".

11.3 What has happened to classification since the Dorking Conference?

Douglas Foskett (1980) mentioned that we gained little from criticisms of any scheme on a purely empirical basis, asking only questions like "What has been omitted?" or "What has been placed in the wrong schedule?" and that this sort of unproductive approach disfigured some of the articles on the "UNISIST Broad System of Ordering". The tendency to pursue specificity alone and to complain of the lack of specificity reflects a serious situation that people are unaware of. Jack Mills (1997) beautifully depicted the present state of retrieval as follows:

"No hope: what was moving was the burgeoning flood of research into an IR which was equated with one particular mode of retrieval – that of specific bits of information, from largely scientific and technical information stores. Simple locating was overwhelmingly predominant as compared with relating. But the two operations – locating and relating – have long been recognized by librarians as the essence of all indexing (… assuming that the first simple locating is insufficient, as in practice it usually is)".

Why is the above plea backed with Mills' practical affairs worth listening to? The answer is that the plea corresponds to an important proposition made by Coates (1960, 19):

"All forms of subject catalogue hold a two-fold objective; first, to enable an enquirer to identify documents on a given subject, and second, to make known the presence of material on allied subjects".

When did the tendency towards the retrieval of "micro- or atomized-information" as called by Mills start? Derek Langridge (1997) said, "By the end of the sixties [in the case of UK] … by the misguided preoccupation with computers". He continued,

"The steady flow of books on classification theory and practice dried up. Organisations that badly needed more effective subject retrieval preferred spending money on computerising their catalogues to improving their classification. The British Library, who had the opportunity to take the lead in sponsoring a modern general classification when its new building was first planned, chose instead to remain a hundred years behind the times. ... Provision of a modern general classification has been left to the Bliss Society [i.e. Bliss Classification Association] with minimal financial support, and apathy from the profession in general".

Maurice Line (1969), later becoming a leading figure of the British Library, stated that the cost of classification was higher than that of cataloguing. The above pleas made by Mills and Langridge were both carried in a commemorative volume published on the occasion of the 1997 London Conference, which was also the sixth and last in the series of the FID/CR's International Study Conference on Classification Research (ISCCR). The first ISCCR was the 1957 Dorking Conference organized by the CRG. The conference was opened with a keynote address given by Ranganathan (1957), which was entitled "Library classification as a discipline", in which he ventured to declare the cost aspect of computerization:

"Machinery can do the work at great speed; but it is more costly, and it requires a vast quantity of minimum turn-out to become economical".

Coates (1997b) in his essay included in the above commemorative volume mentioned that in the intervening 40 years between the 1957 Dorking and 1997 London conferences, the cost aspects as between human and machine handling of information work have been dramatically reversed, concomitantly with a vast increase in potentially accessible information resources. As a result what has been dominant in the information retrieval world is post-coordinate indexing system based on the principle of "simple matching" and "simple coordination" of words or terms found in the text. There has evidently been a decline in the application of classification to libraries and information retrieval, but a decline in quality of retrieval is also unavoidable.

11.4 Two alternative ways forward

According to Coates (1978a), suggestions that classification for information retrieval is obsolete or of dubious utility have come from two quarters: that associated with mechanization, and that associated with system evaluation. The effectiveness of classificatory principles embodied in indexing systems are difficult to measure or likely to be actualized tardily. As Coates and Mills pointed out, a predominance of "short-termism", i.e. short-term cost savings on human intellectual work, could not allow waiting for the probable effectiveness of classification. The effectiveness of classification is not limited to retrieval alone. Mills (2004) mentioned that BSO has been very influential in the development of BC2. If Dahlberg had utilized BSO not "as the basis for a thesaurus" but "as an aid to construction", the result would have been different from the negative one. In this respect, for example, BSO offers the opportunity of enhancing an individual's background knowledge for subject analysis. *The BSO Manual* (Coates, Lloyd and Simandl 1979a, 55-56) said, "Much of the knowledge needed can be gleaned from a fairly superficial inspection of BSO itself. ... For the complexity of the task on hand, this does not seem a very heavy demand upon knowledge and learning capacity". It must be emphasized that background knowledge for subject analysis may be needed not only for classifiers but also for users.

In addition to the decline in quality of retrieval, library and information science (LIS) is now faced with a paradigm shift caused by the following three factors: (1) the likely increase in general accessibility of information sources embracing all fields of knowledge because of the development of the Internet; (2) the popularization of online retrieval by users themselves; and (3) the need for fewer classifiers than before due to central classification services. There are in the main two alternative ways to cope with this paradigm shift. One is the development of search interface software incorporating the technique of artificial intelligence (AI), which Brian and Alina Vickery have already put into practice. In 1986 the Vickerys, together with two young system engineers who were interested in PLEXUS and approached Alina Vickery, established a small software company named Tome Associates Ltd in London, and in 1988 they developed Tome Searcher which was an improved model of PLEXUS (Vickery 1989). The other way forward is to make good use of a fully structured new general classification as a search aid in retrieval and as a teaching aid in general education, the latter of which was suggested by Ranganathan in the keynote address given at the 1957 Dorking Conference mentioned earlier (see also the last paragraph of Section 10.2). In this respect BSO is a new type of information language which was designed for users as well as classifiers (Coates 1995b).

Due to the decline of classification, however strong in technical merit, BSO would not be widely used without a stable institutional support. In this respect the alternative of developing the application of AI technique to classification methods for subject searching may be hopeful. But there is no guarantee that users would be willing to concern themselves with 'concept analysis'. Furthermore, it is true that the currently established general classifications owe their success stories more or less to the decline of classification. In the light of these considerations Coates (1986) left us the following message:

"A healthy profession ought, however, to be more than a passive recipient in these transactions. The technological wave that hit the profession in the 1970s and after has by no means reached its climax, and a major concern of a professional institution should be to identify a revised role for the human element in information handling in relation to standards of professional performance".

12. Conclusion

Within the limits imposed upon it, BSO was designed originally for the specification and ordering of 'blocks of information', with a starting basis in 'institutional warrant' rather than literary warrant. BSO has inherited some of the traditions of library classification, but it also in many respects reflects the work of the CRG (see Endnote 5). The outline of the scheme presents a modern and reasonable world view (see Table 1 and Figure 2). Moreover the schedules are constructed by considering both facets and relations, which means that relational analysis comes back to life in classification (see Table 3). As a result BSO possesses the property of structural 'transparency' and operational 'simplicity', which makes it both 'non-ambiguous' in use and 'predictable' in updating. In the history of library classification there has been no other system than BSO which is designed for users. BSO is an indexing language for users, being a fully structured information language which users can handle with ease.

Acknowledgements

I wish to express my deep gratitude to Dr Leonard Will, formerly of Willpower Information and an erstwhile member of the CRG, for reading the manuscript as a native English speaker and giving valuable advice on the work. Special thanks are due to Ms Yuko Yaguchi, of the Dokkyo Medical University Library, Japan, for technical assistance. In connection with copyright requirements, thanks must be accorded to Emeritus Professor Vanda Broughton, of the Department of Information Studies at University College

London, for giving permission to use relevant illustrations from BSO material.

Endnotes

1. UNISIST was not an official acronym but was a code name for a feasibility study on the establishment of a World Science Information System undertaken jointly by UNESCO and the International Council of Scientific Unions (ICSU). The code name was interpreted as standing for: (1) United Nations Information System in Science and Technology, or (2) Universal System for Information in Science and Technology.

2. The construction of the machine-readable form of the BSO schedules and index owed much to the kind offices of the Bliss Classification Association (BCA). The BCA made available to the BSO Panel the computer programs for BC2, which needed some amendments for BSO.

3. The machine-readable version of BSO originally comprised the following eleven files: BSO10, Title – Technical specification – Issuing body – Copyright; BSO11, List of BSO files; BSO12, Introduction to 1978 edition of BSO; BSO13N, Introduction to 1991 machine-readable version of BSO; BSO14, Combination areas in BSO – Filing order – Combination order – Procedures for combining notation – Examples of notation combinations; BSO15, Optional facet; BSO16, Time facet; BSO17, Place facet including particular countries (ISO 3166 alpha-2 code); BSO18, BSO & the cycle of knowledge – First outline of BSO – Second outline of BSO; BSO20, Full classification schedules; and BSO21, Index to full schedules. BSO10 to BSO18 (Preliminaries) were contained in Disk 1; BSO20 in Disk 2; and BSO21 in Disk 3.

4. The successive members of the BSO Panel since the appointment of the FID/BSO Panel in September 1974 were: (1) Geoffrey Arthur Lloyd (1911-1991) as Rapporteur to August 1977, of the FID Classification Department and formerly of the British Standards Institution; (2) Eric James Coates (1916-2017) as Rapporteur since the latter date, of the British Technology Index and formerly of the British National Bibliography; (3) Dušan Simandl (1924-2006) up to 1984, of the Department of Methodology, Centre of Scientific, Technical and Economic Information (UVTEI), Prague; (4) John Edward Linford (1929-) from 1983, of the European University Institute Library, Florence and formerly of the British National Bibliography; (5) Siniša Maričić (1926-2017) from 1984 up to 1995, of the National and University Library in Zagreb; (6) Colin Neilson as Secretary from 1991, of the Science Museum Library, London; and (7) Keiichi Kawamura as Editorial Consultant from 1995, Japan. The BSO Panel Ltd, UK, was legally dissolved in 2000 when BSO came under the management of UCL/SLAIS (McIlwaine 2000).

5. McIlwaine (2003) mentioned that the "golden age" of the CRG was the 1960s and that "a major milestone in its history" was the 1963 London Conference financed by the NATO grant (Library Association 1963), which resulted in the publication of a 47-page pamphlet (CRG 1964). Unfortunately, the pamphlet including some "far-reaching proposals" has been overlooked as pointed out by McIlwaine and Broughton (2000). At the same conference Coates (1964) gave a paper on a new general classification and foresaw that the outline of the CRG's new general classification to be based on the 'theory of integrative levels' would resemble that of the Bibliographic Classification of Henry Bliss based on the principle of 'gradation by specialities'. The close relation between BSO and the CRG was discussed by Kawamura (2013).

References

BNB. 1963. *Supplementary Classification Schedules: Prepared to Augment the Dewey Decimal Classification for Use in the British National Bibliography and First Introduced in January 1960.* London: Council of the British National Bibliography.

Bertalanffy, Ludwig von. 1968. *General System Theory: Foundations, Development, Applications.* New York: George Braziller.

Brown, Alan G. in collaboration with D.W. Langridge and J. Mills. 1982. *An Introduction to Subject Indexing.* 2nd ed. London: Clive Bingley.

CRG. 1961. "Unique Definition, Fundamental Classes". Classification Research Group Bulletin, no.6. In *Journal of Documentation* 17, no.3: 166-167.

CRG. 1964. *Some Problems of a General Classification Scheme: Report of a Conference held in London, June 1963.* London: Library Association. Reprinted in *Classification and Information Control: Papers Representing the Work of the Classification Research Group during 1960-1968.* London: Library Association, 1969, 7-23.

CRG. 1978. "Broad System of Ordering". Classification Research Group Bulletin, no.11. In *Journal of Documentation* 34, no.1: 42-44.

Coates, Eric J. 1957. "Notation in Classification". In *Proceedings of the International Study Conference on Classification for Information Retrieval held at Beatrice Webb House, Dorking, England, 13th-17th May 1957.* London: Aslib and New York: Pergamon, 51-64.

Coates, Eric J. 1960. *Subject Catalogues: Headings and Structure.* London, Library Association. Reprinted in 1963 and 1969, and reissued with the author's 8-page preface by the same publisher in 1988.

Coates, Eric J. 1964. "CRG Proposals for a New General Classification". Included in Report of the 1963 London Conference (CRG 1964, 38-45). Reprinted in *Classification and Information Control: Papers Representing the Work of the Classification Research Group during 1960-1968.* London: Library Association, 1969, 19-22.

Coates, Eric J. 1968a. "Intermediate Lexicon for Documentation". Classification Research Group Bulletin, no.9. In *Journal of Documentation* 24, no.4: 292-295.

Coates. Eric J. 1968b. "Library Science and Documentation Literature: A New Development in International Co-operation". *Library Association Record* 70, no.7. 178-179.

Coates, Eric J. and David C. Weeks. 1969. *An Outline Intermediate*

Lexicon to Assist Interconversion between Terms Used in Various Indexing Languages in the Field of Scientific and Technical Information Processing. English version. Originally compiled by an International Working Party convened by the Groupe d'Etude sur l'Information Scientifique, Marseilles and Paris, January 1968. Washington, D.C.: George Washington University Medical Center, Biological Sciences Communication Project. For French version, see "GEIS. 1968".

Coates, Eric J. 1970a. "Switching Languages for Indexing". *Journal of Documentation* 26, no.2: 102-110.

Coates, Eric J. 1970b. "British Technology Index". In *Encyclopedia of Library and Information Science*, vol.3, ed. Allen Kent et al. New York: Marcel Dekker, 327-341.

Coates, Eric J. 1973. "Some Properties of Relationships in the Structure of Indexing Languages". *Journal of Documentation* 29, no.4: 390-404.

Coates, Eric J. 1978a. "Classification in Information Retrieval: The Twenty Years Following Dorking". *Journal of Documentation* 34, no.4: 288-299. Reprinted in *From Classification to "Knowledge Organization": Dorking Revisited or "Past is Prelude"*, ed. Alan Gilchrist. FID publication, 714. The Hague: FID, 1997, 11-20.

Coates, Eric J., Geoffrey A. Lloyd and Dusan Simandl. 1978b. *BSO – Broad System of Ordering: Schedule and Index*. 3rd revision. The Hague: FID and Paris: UNESCO. (FID publication, 564). First published version. For French version, see "Coates, Lloyd et Simandl 1981a".

Coates, Eric J., Geoffrey A. Lloyd and Dusan Simandl. 1979a. *The BSO Manual: The Development, Rationale and Use of the Broad System of Ordering*. The Hague: FID. (FID publication, 580).

Coates, Eric J. 1979b. "The Broad System of Ordering". *International Forum on Information and Documentation* 4, no.3: 3-6. Leading paper in a special issue devoted to BSO.

Coates, Eric J. 1980a. "The Broad System of Ordering (BSO)". In *New Trends in Documentation and Information: Proceedings of the 39th FID Congress, University of Edinburgh, 25-28 September 1978*, ed. Peter J. Taylor. FID publication, 566. London: Aslib, 259-273. Rapporteur's first paper on the published version of BSO.

Coates, Eric J. 1980b. *"A Future for BSO?"* A talk given at the BSO Open Meeting, Lyngby, Denmark, 22nd August 1980. Eight-page paper distributed to the attendees.

Coates, Eric J., Geoffry Lloyd et Dusan Simandl. 1981a. *BSO – Système Général de Classement: Tables et Index*, Troisième

Révision. Préparée par le Groupe d'experts FID/BSO. Traduction de la publication FID 564. La Haye: FID et Paris: UNESCO. (PGI/81/ WS/2.0). For original English version, see "Coates, Lloyd and Simandl 1978b".

Coates, Eric J. 1981b. "The Broad System of Ordering: The Compilers Reply to their Critics". *International Forum on Information and Documentation* 6, no.1: 24-30.

Coates, Eric J. 1981c. "Letter to the Editor". *International Classification* 8, no.1: 46.

Coates, Eric J., Geoffrey A. Lloyd and Dusan Simandl. 1981d. *BSO as a Switching Mechanism: Test Exercise – Panel's Report 1981*. Prepared by FID/BSO Panel for FID and UNESCO.

Coates, Eric J., Geoffrey A. Lloyd, Dusan Simandl and John E. Linford. 1985a. *BSO Referral Index: A Subject Index to 36 Data-Bases in the DIALOG System*. Published by FID/BSO Panel for FID and UNESCO. (FID publication, 634).

Coates, Eric J., Geoffrey A. Lloyd, Dusan Simandl and John E. Linford. 1985b. *BSO Referral Test: Panel's Report 1983*. Published by FID/ BSO Panel for FID and UNESCO. (FID publication, 635).

Coates, Eric J. 1986. "FID Broad System of Ordering Panel (FID/BSO): Looking Back 12 Years – and Forward". *International Forum on Information and Documentation* 11, no.3: 64-67.

Coates, Eric J. 1988a. "Ranganathan's Thought and its Significance for the Mechanisation of Information Storage and Retrieval". In *Relevance of Ranganathan's Contributions to Library Science*, ed. T.S. Rajagopalan. New Delhi: Vikas Publishing House, 54-73. Reprinted in *Herald of Library Science* 27, nos.1-2(1988): 3-14. In the reprinted version, besides typos, the original abstract was replaced with different one.

Coates, Eric J. 1988b. "The Role of Classification in Information Retrieval: Action and Thought in the Contribution of Brian Vickery". *Journal of Documentation* 44, no.3: 216-225. Reprinted in *Facets of Knowledge Organization: Proceedings of the ISKO UK Second Biennial Conference, 4th - 5th July 2011, London*, eds. Alan Gilchrist and Judi Vernau. Bingley: Emerald, 2012, 191-202.

Coates, Eric J., John E. Linford, Geoffrey A. Lloyd and Sinisa Maricic. 1991a. *BSO – Broad System of Ordering*. 4th revision. Machine-readable version. St. Albans, UK: BSO Panel Ltd. Published on a set of three 3.5 inch disks. Updated in 1994 and since 2000 the updated version of the 4th revision has been made available online free of charge from the website of University College London: http://www. ucl.ac.uk/fatks/bso.

Coates, Eric J. 1991b. "In Memoriam: Geoffrey Arthur Lloyd". *FID News Bulletin* 41, no.5: 83-84. With a portrait of the deceased. Reprinted without a portrait in *International Classification* 18, no.3 (1991): 166.

Coates, Eric J. 1995a. "BC2 and BSO: Presentation at the Thirty-Sixth Allerton Institute, 1994 Session on Preparing Traditional Classifications for the Future". *Cataloging & Classification Quarterly* 21, no.2: 59-67.

Coates, Eric J. 1995b. "Allerton Institute 1994". *Bliss Classification Bulletin*, no.37: 7-9. http://www.blissclassification.org.uk/B37.pdf.

Coates, Eric J. 1997a. "Subject Searching of Large Scale Information Stores Embracing All Fields of Knowledge: Classification and Concept Matching". In *Knowledge Organization for Information Retrieval: Proceedings of the Sixth International Study Conference on Classification Research held at University College London, 16-18 June 1997*. FID publication, 716. The Hague: FID, 17-22.

Coates, Eric J. 1997b. "1957-1997 *Plus ça Change* ... What Has Happened to Classification since the Dorking Conference?" In *From Classification to "Knowledge Organization": Dorking Revisited or "Past is Prelude"*, ed. Alan Gilchrist. FID publication, 714. The Hague: FID, viii.

Dahlberg, Ingetraut. 1973. *Projekt Ordnungssystem der Wissensgebiete, Phase 1: Materialsammlung; Abschlussbericht und Printouts*. Frankfurt am Main: Deutsche Gesellschaft für Dokumentation.

Dahlberg, Ingetraut. 1980. "The Broad System of Ordering (BSO) as a Basis for an Integrated Social Sciences Thesaurus?" *International Classification* 7, no.2: 66-72.

Dahlberg, Ingetraut. 1996. "Library Catalogs in the Internet: Switching for Future Subject Access". In *Knowledge Organization and Change: Proceedings of the 4th International ISKO Conference, 15-18 July 1996, Washington, DC, USA*, ed. Rebecca Green. *Advances in Knowledge Organization*, 5. Frankfurt am Main: INDEKS Verlag, 155-164.

FID. 1972a. *Introduction to FID's SRC, with Tentative Outline of SRC Superclasses as Agreed by Former FID/CCC/SRC and Presented at the FID/SRC Forum in Budapest, 7th September 1972*.

FID. 1972b. "SRC Forum in Budapest". *FID News Bulletin* 22, no.10: 113.

FID. 1973a. "First Meeting of New FID/SRC Working Group". *FID News Bulletin* 23, no.2: 10-11.

FID. 1973b. "2nd FID/SRC Meeting in The Hague, 26-28 March". *FID News Bulletin* 23, no.4: 45.

FID. 1973c. "3rd FID/SRC Meeting". *FID News Bulletin* 23, no.7: 90.
FID. 1974a. "Subject-Field Reference Code (SRC)". *FID News Bulletin* 24, no.3: 28.
FID. 1974b. "FID/SRC Meeting on Broad System of Ordering". *FID News Bulletin* 24, no.11: 134.
FID. 1975a. "Broad System of Ordering (BSO) for UNISIST". *FID News Bulletin* 25, no.1: 4.
FID. 1975b. "Broad System of Ordering (BSO)". *FID News Bulletin* 25, no.3: 26.
FID. 1977. "Broad System of Ordering (BSO)". *FID News Bulletin* 27, no.4: 40-41.
FID. 1980. "BSO Switching Exercise". *FID News Bulletin* 30, no.1: 1.
FID. 1984a. "Broad System of Ordering". *FID News Bulletin* 34, no.5: 43.
FID. 1984b. *Broad System of Ordering.* The Hague, FID. (FID publication, 638). Four-page publicity leaflet.
FID. 1985. "Broad System of Ordering (BSO)". *FID News Bulletin* 35, no.12: 94.
FID/BSO Panel. 1975. *Outline of Main Subject-Fields for the Broad System of Ordering.* Paris: UNESCO House, May 1975. First provisional draft.
FID/BSO Panel. 1976. *The Broad System of Ordering: 1975 Progress Report.* The Hague: FID Working Group Project under UNESCO Contract, March 1976. First revised draft.
FID/BSO Panel. 1977. *Broad System of Ordering (BSO).* 2nd rev. draft, FID/UNESCO, 30 June 1977. Second revised draft.
Foskett, Antony C. 1979. "The Broad System of Ordering: Old Wine into New Bottles?" *International Forum on Information and Documentation* 4, no.3: 7-12. Included in a special issue devoted to BSO.
Foskett, Douglas J. 1961. "Classification and Integrative Levels". In *The Sayers Memorial Volume: Essays in Honour of William Charles Berwick Sayers*, eds. D.J. Foskett and B.I. Palmer, for the Classification Research Group (London). London: Library Association, 136-150.
Foskett, Douglas J. 1980. "Systems Theory and its Relevance to Documentary Classification". *International Classification* 7, no.1: 2-5.
Fugmann, Robert. 2004. "Learning the Lessons of the Past". In *The History and Heritage of Scientific and Technological Information Systems: Proceedings of the 2002 Conference*, eds. W. Boyd Rayward and Mary Ellen Bowden. Medford, NJ: Information Today,

for the American Society of Information Science and Technology and the Chemical Heritage Foundation, 168-181.

GEIS. 1967. "Informations sur les Techniques Documentaires: Rapport du Groupe d'Etude". *Bulletin des Bibliothèques de France* 12, no.6: 211-238.

GEIS. 1968. *Lexique Intermédiaire*. Marseille: Centre National de la Recherche Scientifique. For English version, see "Coates and Weeks. 1969".

Gardin, Natacha. 1969a. "The Intermediate Lexicon: A New Step towards International Co-operation in Scientific and Technical Information". *Unesco Bulletin for Libraries* 23, no.2: 58-63. For French version, see "Gardin. 1969b".

Gardin, Natacha. 1969b. "Le Lexique Intermédiaire: Un Nouveau Pas vers la Coopération Internationale dans le Domaine de l'Information Scientifique et Technique". *Bulletin de l'Unesco à l'Intention des Bibliothèques* 23, no.2: 66-71. For English version, see "Gardin. 1969a".

Horsnell, Verina. 1974. *Intermediate Lexicon for Information Science: A Feasibility Study; Final Report*. London: Polytechnic of North London, School of Librarianship.

Horsnell, Verina. 1975. "The Intermediate Lexicon: An Aid to International Co-operation". *Aslib Proceedings* 27, no.2: 57-66.

Horsnell, Verina and Alicia Merrett. 1978. *Intermediate Lexicon Research Projects: Phase 2, Evaluation of the Switching Language and Retrieval Performance of the Intermediate Lexicon for Information Science*. London: Polytechnic of North London, School of Librarianship.

International Classification. 1980. "BSO Open Meeting in Copenhagen". *International Classification* 7, no.3: 146.

Kawamura, Keiichi, comp. 2011. *BSO – Broad System of Ordering: An International Bibliography*. Tucson, AZ: University of Arizona Campus Repository. http://hdl.handle.net/10150/129413.

Kawamura, Keiichi. 2013. *BSO, or a New General Classification of the CRG: A Hypothesis and Demonstration* [Text in Japanese with English abstract]. Doctoral thesis accepted by the Osaka City University, Osaka, Japan. (Grant ID: B-2715).

Kawamura, Keiichi. 2018. "Eric Coates". In *ISKO Encyclopedia of Knowledge Organization*, eds. Birger Hjørland and Claudio Gnoli. Updated 2020. https://www.isko.org/cyclo/coates#top.

Kemp, D.A. 1979. Review of "Coates, Lloyd and Simandl 1978b". *Library Review* 28, no.2: 109-110.

Langridge, Derek W. 1997. "A New Dawn?" In *From Classification to*

"Knowledge Organization": Dorking Revisited or "Past is Prelude", ed. Alan Gilchrist. FID publication, 714. The Hague: FID, x.

Library Association. 1963. "Nato [= NATO] Catalogue Conference". *Liaison*, August 1963: 57. *Liaison* was a monthly insertion into the *Library Association Record*.

Line, Maurice B. 1969. "The Cost of Classification: A Note". *Catalogue & Index*, no.16: 4.

Litoukhin, Jury I. 1982. "UNESCO's Project for the Establishment of an Integrated Thesaurus of the Social Sciences". In *The CONTA Conference: Proceedings of the Conference on Conceptual and Terminological Analysis in the Social Sciences held at the Zentrum für Interdisziplinare Forschung (ZIF), Bielefeld, FRG, May 24-27*, ed. Fred W. Riggs. Frankfurt am Main: INDEKS Verlag, 202-206.

Lloyd, Geoffrey A. 1972. "Introduction to the FID's SRC Project". *FID News Bulletin* 22, no.9: 104-105.

Lloyd, Geoffrey A. 1979. *BSO – Broad System of Ordering*. Paper presented at the 45th IFLA Conference held in Copenhagen, Denmark, August 27 – September 1, 1979. Arlington, VA: Educational Resources Information Center. (ERIC document, ED-186 005).

McIlwaine, Ia C. 2000. "Broad System of Ordering". *Newsletter* (IFLA Section on Classification and Indexing), no.22: 20. https://archive.ifla.org/VII/s29/pubs/ci22.pdf.

McIlwaine, Ia C. and Vanda Broughton. 2000. "The Classification Research Group – Then and Now". *Knowledge Organization* 27, no.4: 195-199.

McIlwaine, Ia C. 2003. "Indexing and the Classification Research Group". *Indexer* 23, no.4: 204-208.

Madeley, Hazel. 1983. "The Broad System of Ordering". *Australian Academic & Research Libraries* 14, no.4: 235-246.

Maniez, Jacques. 1997. "Database Merging and the Compatibility of Indexing Languages". *Knowledge Organization* 24, no.4: 213-224.

Mills, Jack. 1997. "Comments on Dorking and After". In *From Classification to "Knowledge Organization": Dorking Revisited or "Past is Prelude"*, ed. Alan Gilchrist. FID publication, 714. The Hague: FID, xi.

Mills, Jack. 2004. "Faceted Classification and Logical Division in Information Retrieval". *Library Trends* 52, no.3: 541-570.

Palnicov, Marat. 1982. "ECSSID WG 3". In *The CONTA Conference: Proceedings of the Conference on Conceptual and Terminological Analysis in the Social Sciences held at the Zentrum für*

Interdisziplinare Forschung (ZIF), Bielefeld, FRG, May 24-27, 1981, ed. Fred W. Riggs. Frankfurt am Main, INDEKS Verlag, 346-348.

Perreault, Jean M. 1979. "Some Problems in the BSO". *International Forum on Information and Documentation* 4, no.3: 16-20. Included in a special issue devoted to BSO.

Ranganathan, S.R. 1955. "Bliss [Obituary]". *Library Association Record* 57, no.9: 374.

Ranganathan, S.R. 1957. "Library Classification as a Discipline". In *Proceedings of the International Study Conference on Classification for Information Retrieval held at Beatrice Webb House, Dorking, England, 13th-17th May 1957*. London: Aslib and New York: Pergamon, 3-12.

Ranganathan, S.R. assisted by M.A. Gopinath. 1967. *Prolegomena to Library Classification*. 3rd ed. Bombay: Asia Publishing House.

Rybatchenkov, Vladimir. 1974. "Development of a Broad System of Ordering for UNISIST Purposes". *International Classification* 1, no.1: 20-21. Abridged version of "UNESCO. 1973".

Soergel, Dagobert. 1979. "The Broad System of Ordering – A Critique". *International Forum on Information and Documentation* 4, no.3: 21-24. Included in a special issue devoted to BSO.

UCL/SLAIS. 2000. *BSO – Broad System of Ordering: A General, Faceted Classification Scheme for Information Exchange and Switching*. London, University College London. http://www.ucl. ac.uk/fatks/bso.

UNESCO and ICSU. 1971. *UNISIST: Study Report on the Feasibility of a World Science Information System*. Paris: UNESCO.

UNESCO. 1972. *UNISIST, Broad System of Ordering: Preliminary Remarks from Unesco, Presented at FID/SRC Forum, Budapest, 7th September 1972*.

UNESCO. 1973. "Development of a Broad System of Ordering for UNISIST Purposes". *UNISIST Newsletter* 1, no.2: 3-4. For abridged version, see "Rybatchenkov. 1974".

UNESCO. 1975. "Broad System of Ordering – Progress Report". *UNISIST Newsletter* 3, no.2: 5-6.

Vickery, Alina, H.M. Brooks, B.A. Robinson and B.C. Vickery. 1986. *Expert System for Referral: Final Report of the First Phase of the Project*. London: University of London Central Information Service. (British Library Research and Development Report, 5924).

Vickery, Alina, H.M. Brooks, B.A. Robinson, J. Stephens and B.C. Vickery. 1988. *Expert System for Referral*. London: British Library. (Library and Information Research Report, 66).

Vickery, Alina. 1989. "The Experience of Building Expert Search Systems". In *Online Information 88: 12th International Online Information Meeting: London, 6-8 December 1988*, vol.1. Oxford: Learned Information, 301-313.

Vickery, Brian C., Margaret Slater, Alexandra Presanis and Rose Reynolds. 1969. *Classification in Science Information: A Comparative Study Undertaken by Aslib for the International Council of Scientific Unions as a Contribution to the ICSU/UNESCO Study of the Feasibility of a World Science Information System (UNISIST)*. London: Aslib. (Document UNISIST/CSI/5.8) (ERIC document, ED 061 955).

Vickery, Brian C. and Ia C. McIlwaine. 1979. "Structuring and Switching: A Discussion of the Broad System of Ordering". *International Forum on Information and Documentation* 4, no.3: 13-15. Included in a special issue devoted to BSO.

Wellisch, Hans H. 1979. "The Broad System of Ordering, or Bishop Wilkins Redivivus: A Review Article". *Library Quarterly* 49, no.4: 444-452.

Wells, Arthur James. 1957. "British National Bibliography". *Annals of Library Science* 4, no.3: 73-89.

Index

[著者紹介]

川村敬一（かわむら・けいいち）

1948　青森市に生まれる
1972　神奈川大学経済学部卒業
1976　図書館短期大学別科修了
職歴　元獨協医科大学図書館
　　　大正大学司書講習講師，淑徳大学兼任講師，
　　　英国 BSO 委員会編集顧問などを兼任
学位　博士（創造都市）大阪市立大学
近著　『三訂情報資源組織演習』（分担）樹村房，2021
　　　『主題検索の現状理解と今後の方向性について』樹村房，2020
　　　"Eric Coates". *ISKO Encyclopedia of Knowledge Organization*, 2018
　　　Bibliography of the British Technology Index. Tokyo: Jusonbo, 2015
　　　『BSO, あるいは CRG の新一般分類表：仮説と論証』博士論文，2013
　　　BSO – Broad System of Ordering: an international bibliography. Tucson,
　　　　　AZ: University of Arizona Campus Repository, 2011 ほか
受賞　Satija Research Foundation for Library & Information Science (SRFLIS)
　　　　　Lifetime Achievement Award, 2020
　　　第 21 回図書館サポートフォーラム賞，2019

Broad System of Ordering（BSO）

2023 年 8 月 29 日　初版第 1 刷発行

〈検印廃止〉

著　　者　　川　村　敬　一

発 行 者　　大　塚　栄　一

発 行 所　　株式会社　樹村房

〒 112-0002
東京都文京区小石川 5 丁目 11-7
電　話　　03-3868-7321
Ｆ Ａ Ｘ　　03-6801-5202
振　替　　00190-3-93169
https://www.jusonbo.co.jp/

表紙デザイン／原　美穂
組版・印刷・製本／株式会社丸井工文社

Bibliography of the British Technology Index

Compiled by
Keiichi Kawamura

British Technology Index (BTI) was commenced by the Library Association (LA), London, in 1962. It was a monthly and annual subject guide to articles in about 400 British technical journals. BTI introduced new indexing techniques, the principle of which had been discussed by the first editor Eric Coates in his *Subject catalogues: headings and structure* (London, LA, 1960). The Society of Indexers considered BTI "an indexing masterpiece" in the field of science, and some people called Coates "the genius of subject indexing".

The bibliography lists about 320 references to BTI ranging from 1958 to 2015. Eight languages are concerned with the bibliography: English, Finnish, French, German, Hungarian, Japanese, Spanish and Swedish. Every item has an English abstract. Items are arranged in systematic order, and cross-references among related items as well as author and language indexes complement the systematic arrangement. Appended is a title list of Coates' BTI-related works arranged in chronological order.

Tokyo: Jusonbo, 2015, 123p. 30 cm.
ISBN978-4-88367-250-9. 3,000 yen + tax.

〒112-0002 東京都文京区小石川5-11-7 　樹村房　TEL：03-3868-7321 FAX：03-6801-5202
URL：https://www.jusonbo.co.jp/ 　　　　　　　E-mail：webinfo@jusonbo.co.jp